THE GOSPEL PREACHED THROUGH MUSIC

THE GOSPEL PREACHED THROUGH MUSIC

The Purpose and Practice of Lutheran Church Music

By
Daniel Zager

The Good Shepherd Institute
Concordia Theological Seminary Press
Fort Wayne, Indiana

Cover Image:
Trumpets, Stained Glass
Chapel of Christ Triumphant
Concordia University Wisconsin

Used by permission

ISBN 978-0-9615927-2-1

© 2013 The Good Shepherd Institute
Concordia Theological Seminary Press
6600 North Clinton Street
Fort Wayne, Indiana 46825

Cover Design: Steve Blakey, BB Design
Printed on acid-free paper in the United States of America.
Set in Adobe Book Antiqua.
Manufactured by Dataprint in Fort Wayne, Indiana.

CONTENTS

ILLUSTRATIONS

Examples

Figure

PREFACE

This small book is about the purpose and practice of music in Lutheran worship. The content — more conceptual than strictly historical or practical — is prompted in part by the debates on worship and music that have taken place in American Lutheranism from the 1970s on, debates that continue even to today.

This book is also prompted by my belief that Lutheran church musicians must think more carefully about the *purpose* of music in worship. I believe that we can learn much on that topic from Martin Luther and from the work of Lutheran cantors active during the first three centuries of Lutheranism. A higher view of the purpose of music in Lutheran worship will inform our *practice* of Lutheran church music, including our *choices* of music for each Sunday and festival of the church year. Thus, my intended audience for this book includes Lutheran church musicians and their pastoral colleagues, who share the high responsibility for determining what music is fitting within each Divine Service.

Central to my thinking about church music is the premise that music itself is never neutral, that music always carries meaning. While that is hardly a startling proposition in the broader world of musical thought, it has necessarily been denied in certain quarters of the church for at least the past three decades. In so doing, pastors, church musicians, and laity alike have sought to advance an agenda that any musical language and expression, any musical style, can be used in the church — because music is neutral and only verbal texts bear meaning. That false premise will be explored further in this book.

While it is impossible to discuss church music without referring to worship, I consciously try here to focus primarily on music. Worship is a theological topic treated most comprehensively by theologians. As a

ix

musicologist and a Lutheran church musician, my focus quite naturally is on music, with some attention to matters of worship and liturgy — the contexts in which Lutheran church music takes place.

Martin Luther observed that "God has preached the gospel through music too."[1] That concept stands as a summary for why I wanted to write this book. Too often I see Lutheran church musicians and pastors who are unfamiliar with Luther's premise. Without a sense of that high purpose for music in Lutheran worship, the practice of Lutheran church music is too often less than it could be, with the treasures of Lutheran music too frequently ignored, and the people deprived of singing and hearing what is an exceptional body of theologically rich music that proclaims the Word of God. I write to encourage a widespread recovery of and recommitment to the amazing potential of Lutheran church music, for "God has preached the gospel through music too."

*   *   *

I extend my thanks to four friends who generously took time to read this book in its earliest manuscript form: Bryan Gerlach, Robin Leaver, Richard Resch, and Jon Vieker. I benefited very much from their reactions and critical comments; they, however, bear no responsibility for errors in fact or other shortcomings in the published book. I am also grateful to Constance Buszin Seddon, who edited the book with her customary expertise and with her keen understanding of Lutheran church music. Steve Blakey produced the book and brought to this task the same expertise in design and production that has characterized all of his work with the publications of The Good Shepherd Institute. Finally, I thank Richard Resch, Co-Director of The Good Shepherd Institute of Concordia Theological Seminary, Fort Wayne, Indiana, for including this book in the publication program of the Institute.

Note

1   Martin Luther, Table Talk, ed. Theodore G. Tappert, Luther's Works, vol. 54 (Philadelphia: Fortress Press, 1967), 129.

ABBREVIATIONS

BWV   [Bach-Werke-Verzeichnis] Wolfgang Schmieder, ed., *Thematisch-systematisches Verzeichnis der musikalischen Werke von Johann Sebastian Bach: Bach-Werke-Verzeichnis (BWV)*, 2d ed. (Wiesbaden: Breitkopf und Härtel, 1990).

CW   *Christian Worship: A Lutheran Hymnal* (Milwaukee: Northwestern Publishing House, 1993)

ELH   *Evangelical Lutheran Hymnary* (St. Louis: MorningStar Music Publishers, 1996)

ELW   *Evangelical Lutheran Worship* (Minneapolis: Augsburg Fortress Publishers, 2006)

FC   Formula of Concord

LSB   *Lutheran Service Book* (St. Louis: Concordia Publishing House, 2006)

LW   Luther's Works: American Edition, 55 vols. (St. Louis: Concordia Publishing House; Philadelphia/Minneapolis: Muhlenberg/Fortress Press, 1955–1986)

SC   Small Catechism

SWV   [Schütz-Werke-Verzeichnis] Werner Bittinger, ed., *Schütz-Werke-Verzeichnis: Kleine Ausgabe (SWV)* (Kassel: Bärenreiter, 1960)

TLH   *The Lutheran Hymnal* (St. Louis: Concordia Publishing House, 1941)

INTRODUCTION

The Debates about Lutheran Worship and Music

Since the 1970s, Lutherans in America have witnessed, and some have participated in, protracted and vigorous debates concerning the meaning, purpose, and practice of worship. By no means limited to Lutheranism, such debates have, in fact, taken place in many corners of American Christendom.[1] Sometimes characterized as "worship wars," the debates at times became acrimonious and in that regard antithetical to Psalm 133:1 ("Behold, how good and pleasant it is when brothers dwell in unity!"). But there has also been a more salutary effect. These debates required us to think much more deeply and critically about worship, about the theology of Lutheran worship, and about the broad spectrum of worship viewpoints and practices that we hear and see around us within American Lutheranism.[2] Interestingly, these debates have taken place at precisely the time that the Internet and various forms of electronic communication have developed and flourished. Thus, one engaged the debate not only by reading books or journal and newspaper articles, but also by participating in e-mail discussion lists or by reading and reacting to online blogs. Further, congregational Web sites have offered rich possibilities to observe what Lutheran churches throughout America are thinking about worship. While nothing can replace actual participation in, or on-site observation of, worship in Lutheran churches, congregational Web sites often provide opportunities to peruse Sunday bulletins online or to read local statements about worship theologies and practices. In that sense, church Web sites are, in effect, primary source documents, as they testify to the broad range of worship theologies and practices in Lutheran congregations.

In these written and online debates about worship in American Lutheranism, matters of *music* have frequently loomed large. In fact, matters of music have often been at the very center of the debates about Lutheran worship practices. Particularly in the more theologically conservative branches of American Lutheranism, pastors who advocated change in worship practices—for the sake of *growth* in worship attendance—regarded music as an aspect of worship that was not only permissible to change, but actually ripe for adjustment and change. Such pastors might conceptualize the content of their preaching as theological *substance* that should not change, but music and liturgy were deemed matters merely of *style* that could and perhaps should change.[3] To alter in any substantial way the theological content of Lutheran preaching would be to invite charges of heresy, but to change Lutheran worship music—away from its historical roots in the church and toward a new model based on the pop music of the 1960s and beyond—was deemed safe (in the sense of being nonheretical) and, moreover, effective in bringing more people to attend worship. Of course, this distinction between substance and style depended on the erroneous view that Lutheran church music itself is nonsubstantive—that the hymn texts of the church play no part in theological proclamation and that the hymnic, choral, and instrumental music of the church has no capacity to signal either meaning or identity. Thus, worship music became a convenient change agent within the larger strategies of church growth, with Lutheran churches that embraced church growth philosophies and procedures thereby inheriting decidedly non-Lutheran views on the purpose and practice of church music.

While music has often been central to the worship debates in American Lutheranism, theological discussions that attempted to ameliorate disagreements on matters of worship might ignore considerations of music entirely. For example, the Council of Presidents of The Lutheran Church—Missouri Synod (LCMS) approved a set of "Theses on Worship" in September 2009.[4] For all of the debates within the LCMS about the purpose and practice of music within worship, this document had nothing to say about music. While on the surface that might seem curious—rather like ignoring an elephant in the room—there is a perfectly plausible reason why this document had nothing to say about music in Lutheran worship. This group of LCMS pastors quite understandably approached their difficult task as Lutheran theologians should—they searched Scripture and the Lutheran Confessions for principles that might shed theological light on the ongoing, vigorous debates within the LCMS on worship. Their primary task was to consider "the diversity of worship practices in LCMS congregations"[5] in the context of a distinctly Lutheran theology of worship—a topic that can be informed only by Scripture and the Confessions.

But *music* is not a primary focus of either Scripture or the Confessions. More precisely, neither the Bible nor the Lutheran Confessions speaks directly to the kinds of questions raised by the varied musical practices we see around us in Lutheran congregations of the early twenty-first century,

2

questions such as: Is it a good choice to employ the pop music idioms of our day in Lutheran worship? Is it a good choice to diminish or even abandon the Lutheran heritage of church music (music composed from the sixteenth century up to and including the present day) and instead borrow heavily from the "worship and praise" genres of twentieth- and twenty-first-century American evangelical, pentecostal, or nondenominational churches? What are the implications of overlaying a supposed Lutheran theology with distinctly non-Lutheran musical expressions? Neither the Bible nor the Lutheran Confessions will shed direct light on such questions that relate to worship music and Lutheran identity. Thus, it is no surprise that the LCMS "Theses on Worship," as well as the papers subsequently presented at a January 2010 LCMS "Model Theological Conference on Worship," have almost nothing to say about music, even though questions concerning music loom very large indeed in the ongoing Lutheran debates on worship.[6] Where then might one turn for perspectives on and answers to questions regarding music in Lutheran worship?

Before considering that question directly, recall the assertion above, namely that "music . . . is not a primary focus of either Scripture or the Confessions." If that is true, then might we not be at liberty to use whatever kind of music we want in Lutheran worship? Might that be the reason why the LCMS Council of Presidents did not speak to matters of music in worship? Absent specific guidance *on music* from Scripture and the Confessions could it be that there is nothing to say about the purpose and practice of music in worship? The debate about music in Lutheran worship has sometimes been framed around questions of what is *permissible*, but it may be more useful to frame the issues around a different question: Is this music an apt and *fitting* choice? Does this music—and here I really mean music, not text—stand well alongside Lutheran theology? Is this music a good match for Lutheran theology as it is expressed in orders of service, preaching, and hymnody? Thus, we ask better questions—and obtain better answers—when we ask not what is permitted but rather what is truly fitting for the proclamation of God's Word. With the Apostle Paul, we might say: "'All things are lawful,' but not all things are helpful. 'All things are lawful,' but not all things build up" (1 Cor 10:23).

Let's explore further the premise that Scripture does not speak directly to our twenty-first-century questions about music in Lutheran worship. Note what I did in the previous paragraph: I invoked a scriptural passage from one of Paul's epistles to assist in making the point that when I ask questions about music in Lutheran worship I prefer to ask which musical practices constitute good choices (i.e., what is "helpful" and what "builds up") rather than attempting to codify what is permitted ("lawful"). But Paul, of course, was not writing about music in worship. So I invoke this passage not to suggest that it provides a scriptural answer to a twenty-first-century question about music in Lutheran worship, but to proceed by way of a relevant biblical analogy. In other words, I did not invoke a passage of Scripture to "prove a point" concerning music in worship. Indeed, because the purpose of Scripture is to make us "wise for salvation" (2 Tm 3:15) we should not expect it to assist in answering specific questions—much less in "clinching" arguments—concerning the place of music in twenty-first-century Lutheran worship.

Scripture, of course, includes oft-quoted passages that seem to speak to matters of music. For example, the psalmist's injunction to "Sing a new song" (Ps 33:3, 96:1, 98:1, 144:9, 149:1) has at times in the worship and music debates been used to justify the singing of "contemporary" worship and praise songs—the "new songs"—in Lutheran worship. But as *The Lutheran Study Bible* aptly points out in its introduction to the Book of Psalms:

> The "old song" was the Song of Moses, which celebrated the redemption from Egypt (Ex 15:1–18). The "new song" in the Psalms often celebrated redemption from exile (cf Ne 12:27). Rv 5:8–9 says the "new song" is about the final redemption through Jesus.[7]

Similarly, the Greek church father Clement of Alexandria (ca. 150–ca. 215) referred to Jesus as "the New Song":

> He who is from David, yet before him, the Word of God . . . This is the New Song, the shining manifestation among us now of the Word, who was in the beginning and before the beginning.[8]

Thus, we err by positing a one-to-one correspondence between the psalmist's "new song" and the worship and praise genres of late twentieth-century American evangelicalism.

Similarly, Ephesians 5:19 and Colossians 3:16, with their references to "psalms and hymns and spiritual songs," have been invoked as a reason to add "praise songs" to the psalms and hymns already sung in Lutheran worship. The problem is that we have no way of knowing precisely what Paul was referring to by the words that have customarily been translated as "spiritual songs," and Paul, of course, was referring to literary types rather than to musical styles.

If Scripture does not provide precise answers for our questions regarding music in twenty-first-century Lutheran worship, what about the Lutheran Confessions? Might they provide answers to music-related questions? The Confessions have much to say about worship, but nothing specifically about music. See, for example, the "Subject Index" in either the Kolb/Wengert edition or the revised Dau/Bente edition of *The Book of Concord*. In neither index does one find an entry for music, though both have entries for "Worship."[9] Further, the Confessions have much to say about ceremonies, human traditions, and *adiaphora*—matters "that are neither commanded nor forbidden in God's word but that were introduced in the churches for the sake of good order and decorum." Article X of the *Formula of Concord* ("Concerning Ecclesiastical Practices Which Are Called Adiaphora or Indifferent Matters") is of particular importance.[10] Lutheran debates about worship in the late twentieth and early twenty-first centuries have necessarily addressed adiaphora, though at times in a rather careless way that equates adiaphora with a spirit of "anything goes." But the concept of adiaphora was never intended as a sanction for license or for carelessness, as Daniel G. Reuning has observed:

> As much as Luther and other contributors to the Book of Concord insisted that music was an adiaphoron, they were just as insistent that music was, nonetheless, not a matter of indifference, but a matter that required both theological and musical judgment. . . .[11]

Suffice it to say in the present context that the Confessions do not provide twenty-first-century Lutherans with answers to questions about the purpose and practice of Lutheran church music.

After these brief excursions into the question of whether Scripture or the Confessions will "shed direct light on such questions that relate to worship music and Lutheran identity" (p. 3 above), we return to the question posed earlier: "Where then might we turn for perspectives on and answers to questions regarding music in Lutheran worship?" Absent guidance from Scripture and the Confessions, Martin Luther's (1483–1546) writings on music in worship are foundational for an inquiry regarding the purpose and practice of Lutheran church music. Further, Lutheran church musicians of the twenty-first century gain valuable insights by turning to some of their most illustrious predecessors, such as Michael Praetorius (1571–1621), Heinrich Schütz (1585–1672), and Johann Sebastian Bach (1685–1750). The goal in what follows is to use their writings, their music, and details of their careers as guides to two questions with which we twenty-first-century Lutheran church musicians must grapple: What is the *purpose* of music in twenty-first-century Lutheran worship? What should be the central defining characteristics of the *practice* of music in twenty-first-century Lutheran worship? What I am suggesting here is that we can learn from history and from these Lutheran cantors important *guiding principles* of Lutheran church music. I am emphatically *not* suggesting that the way to resolve debates on music in Lutheran worship is to limit our music-making to repertories from the first three centuries of Lutheranism. The distinction between guiding principles and historic repertories is critical to what follows, the former being of first importance here.

Notes

1 For a view from outside of Lutheranism, see Charles Trueheart, "Welcome to the Next Church," *The Atlantic Monthly* (August 1996): 37–58.

2 For a recent Lutheran overview of worship and liturgy, see Timothy C. J. Quill, "Liturgical Worship," in *Perspectives on Christian Worship: 5 Views*, ed. J. Matthew Pinson (Nashville: Broadman and Holman Academic, 2009), 18–81.

3 See, for example, David S. Luecke, *Evangelical Style and Lutheran Substance: Facing America's Mission Challenge* (St. Louis: Concordia Publishing House, 1988); and Luecke, *Apostolic Style and Lutheran Substance: Ten Years of Controversy Over What Can Change* (Lima, Ohio: Fairway Press, 1999).

4 The Lutheran Church—Missouri Synod, "Theses on Worship," http://www.lcms.org/page.aspx?pid=726&DocID=1058.

5 Ibid., quoted from cover letter of Rev. Gerald B. Kieschnick, then President of the LCMS.

6 The Lutheran Church—Missouri Synod, Commission on Worship, papers from January 2010 "Model Theological Conference on Worship," http://www.lcms.org/page.aspx?pid=696. For a published summary of this conference, see Barry L. Bobb, "Toward a Theology of Worship That Is . . . ," *Cross Accent: Journal of the Association of Lutheran Church Musicians* 18:2 (2010): 5–11.

7 *The Lutheran Study Bible: English Standard Version* (St. Louis: Concordia Publishing House, 2009), 843.

8 *Music in Early Christian Literature*, ed. James McKinnon, Cambridge Readings in the Literature of Music (Cambridge: Cambridge University Press, 1987), 30. See also the excerpt from Clement of Alexandria as translated in Oliver Strunk, *Source Readings in Music History: Antiquity and the Middle Ages* (New York: W. W. Norton, 1965), 62–63: "the Christ—I have called Him a New Song" (p. 63).

9 *The Book of Concord: The Confessions of the Evangelical Lutheran Church*, ed. Robert Kolb and Timothy J. Wengert (Minneapolis: Fortress Press, 2000). This volume is subsequently cited as: Kolb/Wengert. *Concordia, The Lutheran Confessions: A Reader's Edition of the Book of Concord*, ed. Paul Timothy McCain, 2d ed. (St. Louis: Concordia Publishing House, 2006). A useful resource is James L. Brauer, *Worship, Gottesdienst, Cultus Dei: What the Lutheran Confessions Say About Worship* (St. Louis: Concordia Publishing House, 2005).

10 Kolb/Wengert, FC 515–16, 635–40.

11 Daniel G. Reuning, "Confessional Music," *Concordia Theological Quarterly* 44 (October 1980): 213–14.

1

THE PURPOSE OF LUTHERAN CHURCH MUSIC

Attracting people, praising God, proclaiming the Word of God — all of these phrases have been used to define the purpose of music in Lutheran worship. Different understandings of the purpose of music in worship have led to differences in the practice of music within Lutheran worship, a phenomenon that has become abundantly clear during the debates on music and worship of the late twentieth and early twenty-first centuries.

Attracting People

What is the purpose of music in Lutheran worship? Some pastors and musicians have desired to use music as the primary means of attracting people to worship. One Lutheran pastor, for example, asserts that "Contemporary music — pop, rock, country/western, rap — continue to be the heart language of today's generations. As people shop for a church, they look for congregations that value them by valuing their music. In designing worship services attractive to today's consumers, no factor has greater impact than the choice of music."[1] This understanding of the purpose of music in Lutheran worship allows for almost any kind of music — whatever works to attract people. One Lutheran church musician wrote about the use of "music preference surveys," the premise being that a congregation should understand the musical preferences of the surrounding community as well as its own members. There are three questions suggested for the music preference survey:

1. What are three radio stations you've set on your car stereo's preset buttons?
2. What is your favorite kind of music?
3. Who are your favorite artists or bands?

The congregation used the results of the survey to craft a "music mission statement": "We will shape our repertoire with songs that can be presented to the congregation in the musical genres of soft rock, country, and contemporary acoustic."[2] Those three genres were the majority preferences identified by the surveys, music in those styles thus being considered optimal for the purpose of attracting more people to attend worship. While music in those particular styles is used to attract people to hear the Gospel, there is no claim for music playing a role in actually proclaiming the Gospel.

Praising God

What is the purpose of music in Lutheran worship? Perhaps the most frequent answer to the question goes something like this: "With our music we give praise and thanks to God." While that answer is not wrong, it is incomplete and therefore not fully adequate. The problem with the answer is that it is stated from our human point of view. Arthur A. Just Jr. observes that "Lutherans seldom begin theology from below, from man's perspective, but from above, from God's perspective."[3] Thus, a theology of worship — including the role and purpose of music in Lutheran worship — starts not with what we do, i.e., *we* give praise and thanks to our God, but rather with what God does, as He gives His gifts through His Divine Service to His people. There is a rhythm, an order that is essential to understand: 1) God gives His gifts of forgiveness and salvation through His Word and His Sacraments, 2) we respond in thanks and praise, in part through music.[4] But music is not limited to the second part of this equation — our response in thanks and praise. Music is also connected with the proclamation of His Word; that is to say, the gift of His Word may be clothed in music. One has only to think of the myriad musical settings of any one of the psalms, or of Mary's Magnificat, or Simeon's Nunc dimittis. But in addition to the psalms and biblical canticles, a hymn, such as Martin Luther's "Dear Christians, One and All, Rejoice," while not drawn word for word from Scripture, still bears God's Word. In the first volume of his monumental treatise *Syntagma Musicum* (1615), the Lutheran cantor Michael Praetorius commented on Luther's hymn: "And in this song, all the merit of Christ, etc., is contained."[5] Of this hymn, the German Lutheran theologian Oswald Bayer wrote:

> In a dramatic hymn Luther sang of the fact that God's being is gift and promise. This hymn, "Dear Christians, One and All," is the most telling and appropriate confession of the triune God that I know. . . . What takes place in this drama is our justification. . . . Justification comes when God himself enters the deadly dispute of "justifications," suffers from it, carries it out in himself. He does this through the death of his Son, which is also God's own death. In this way God takes the dispute into himself and overcomes it on our behalf.

The whole being of God is understood as a self-giving promise that is made to us by the Son in our lost estate when we were given over to death: "Stay close to me. . . . Your ransom I myself will be" (verses 7–10). What a promise is this! It must surely cause us to sing.[6]

Bayer is right—this great promise, this great gift of God, does cause us to sing, and when we do so via Luther's hymn we are engaged in proclaiming God's Word—to one another in the Christian congregation and to the world around us. Thus, we err when we consign music only to the category of praise; praise is not the sole or even primary purpose of music in Lutheran worship.

Proclaiming the Word of God

What is the purpose of music in Lutheran worship? The primary purpose of music in Lutheran worship is to proclaim the Word of God. In an important statement that is too often overlooked—and counterintuitive to the prevailing generic-Protestant thinking on music and praise, Luther suggested that "proclaiming [the Word of God] through music" is, in fact, the way that we praise God:

> After all, the gift of language combined with the gift of song was only given to man to let him know that he should praise God with both word and music, namely, by proclaiming [the Word of God] through music and by providing sweet melodies with words.[7]

Luther posits first of all that the way to praise God is by proclaiming His Word. This distinctive insight stands in contrast to the more customary concepts of praise, in which humans "ascribe worth to" (i.e., "worship") God. Luther moves beyond this anthropocentric model by stressing that we truly praise God when we proclaim His work of salvation in His Son—a Christological model of praise that is centered on God and His work rather than on man.[8] Luther provides yet another foundational insight when he joins *music* to this notion of praising by proclaiming. Thus, he links music directly with proclamation.

One way to answer the question "What is the purpose of music in Lutheran worship?" is this: For Lutherans the purpose of music is to proclaim the Word of God, which is the way we praise God, and when that proclamation and praise takes place through music that is well made and skillfully rendered, people will be attracted to the church's worship. The order of elements is crucial here. It is not that we begin by using music to attract people—so that they might participate in sung praise (in fact, the non-Christian—so often the target of "contemporary praise services"—is unable to praise a God s/he has not yet come to know, cf. 1 Cor 2:14).[9] The order is precisely the opposite: 1) Music plays its part in proclaiming the good news of salvation through Christ, 2) this proclamation is itself the highest act of praise (i.e., as the Lutheran congregation sings a hymn such as "Dear Christians, One and All, Rejoice" it is engaged *simultaneously* in proclamation and praise), and 3) it is this pattern of proclamation/praise that ultimately serves to attract people to the church and its message. John Kleinig puts the proposition this way:

> God does not need us to flatter him, but he does want us to tell others about his goodness, so that they too will put their trust in him and enjoy his good gifts. And that is what we do when we praise him in songs that proclaim his goodness.[10]

We don't start with ourselves, using music as a "draw" for the "unchurched"; rather, it all begins with God and His Word (His gifts, His grace, His gracious invitation, His Divine Service to us), the proclamation of which — for Lutherans — often employs music.

But, one may ask, what kind of music? And what about that phrase "music that is *well made*"? By what criteria does one define "well made"? And who defines "well made" with regard to the music used in Lutheran worship? Such questions are central to the ongoing debates concerning Lutheran worship and music, and too often such questions are answered in ways that deny the church's own lengthy and rich history of music. Within the worship and music debates it sometimes seems as if the church exists only in the here and now, with no *historical* context — no musical past of its own, no usable musical traditions, and no shared sense of what constitutes music of, by, and for the church. Moreover, within these debates one often looks in vain for even the barest sense of a *functional* context — that music should find its place within the church's own sense of ordered time, as determined by the church year calendar and the weekly and daily round of orders of service, and that music should find its place in the theological context established by the lectionary. How do we determine what music is "well made"? We study and sing the music that has been created *within the church's own musical culture* down through the ages — from medieval chant, to Renaissance polyphony, to the Gospel motets, cantatas, and organ chorale preludes of the musical Baroque, to the choral and organ works of nineteenth-century composers, to the liturgical *Gebrauchsmusik* (i.e., functional music) of the twentieth century. These historical repertories provide flesh for the concept of "well made" music, and they become the measuring tools by which we appraise the worth of newly composed music and the potential of such new music to participate in proclamation of the Gospel.

What follows in this chapter is a further investigation of Luther's views on music as proclamation. Luther provided the foundation that enabled composers such as Michael Praetorius, Heinrich Schütz, and J. S. Bach (among many others — including living composers of our day) to proclaim the Word of God through music. Exploring the writings, pertinent career circumstances, and (in Chapter Two) the music of these Lutheran cantors provides a concrete way of examining Lutheran church music as proclamation of the Word of God.

Martin Luther (1483–1546) on the Purpose of Music in Worship

Martin Luther's distinctive insight on proclamation and praise through music (quoted above) came from his preface to a 1538 multi-composer anthology of Latin polyphonic music for Lutheran worship — the *Symphoniae Iucundae*, published by his Wittenberg coworker Georg Rhau (1488-1548), an important and prolific printer and publisher during the early decades of the German Reformation. ("Polyphonic" refers to a musical texture in which two or more independent voices are combined to form a harmonious whole; "monophonic" refers to a single voice, as, for example, Latin chant or a hymn tune without harmonization.) While that specific insight by Luther is particularly foundational in defining a theology of Lutheran church music, it is by no means his only recorded thought on the purpose of music in the worship of the church. In fact, in this same preface Luther pronounced music "an excellent gift of God"[11] and stated that "next to the Word of God, music deserves the highest praise."[12] He went on to say that "The Holy Ghost himself honors her [i.e., music] as an instrument for his proper work . . . ."[13] In his Small Catechism Luther succinctly defined the work of the Holy Spirit:

> . . . the Holy Spirit has called me through the gospel, enlightened me with his gifts, made me holy and kept me in the true faith, just as he calls, gathers, enlightens, and makes holy the whole Christian church on earth and keeps it with Jesus Christ in the one common, true faith.[14]

When we combine those two statements, we see that Luther links music, "an instrument for his [i.e., the Holy Spirit's] proper work" to the proclamation of the Gospel ("the Holy Spirit has called me through the gospel"). Thus, Luther defined a high purpose for music in worship — as an instrument of the Holy Spirit, for the proclamation of the Gospel.

In an earlier preface to a collection of German-language polyphony, Johann Walter's (1496-1570) *Geystliche gesangk Buchleyn* of 1524, Luther anthropocentric =

summarized why he and others had written hymn texts and tunes: "so that the holy gospel which now by the grace of God has risen anew may be noised and spread abroad."[15] In that preface Luther went on to declare: "But I would like to see all the arts, especially music, used in the service of Him who gave and made them."[16] Luther was very clear—his hymn texts and tunes in whatever guise, sung monophonically or polyphonically, are for the purpose of proclaiming the Gospel, that the Gospel "may be noised and spread abroad."

In another important statement, the preface to the 1545 *Geystliche Lieder*—published by Valentin Babst in Leipzig and sometimes referred to as the "Babst Gesangbuch"—Luther again wrote about the purpose of hymns:

> For God has cheered our hearts and minds through his dear Son, whom he gave for us to redeem us from sin, death, and the devil. He who believes this earnestly cannot be quiet about it. But he must gladly and willingly sing and speak about it so that others also may come and hear it.[17]

Note that Luther places "singing" and "speaking" the Gospel on the same plane, as he also does, for example, in the first stanza of his Christmas hymn "Vom Himmel hoch, da komm' ich her" ("From Heaven Above to Earth I Come"): "Davon ich *sing'n* und *sagen* will" ("Whereof I now will sing and speak"). What should we sing about? Luther made clear that we should sing about Christ, our redeemer from sin, death, and the devil. Luther also spoke to the question of *why* we sing proclamatory hymns of Christ: "so that others also may come and hear it." Thus, for Luther, the *confessional* content or substance of hymns is the reason for their *missional* value—accomplished through the purpose of hymnody as sung proclamation. Luther's Christocentric emphasis with regard to hymn texts stands as an important guideline for the twenty-first-century Lutheran pastor and church musician, both of whom live in a culture inundated with self-focused, inward-looking religious song. Pastors and church musicians will separate out those anthropocentric songs that do not sing of Christ, and *teach why* hymn texts that proclaim the Word of God are superior to religious songs that have an inward curve, that focus on man's feelings and his perceived needs.

In some of his correspondence Luther also wrote cogently about the purpose of music. As he was beginning to compile hymn texts and tunes in 1523, he wrote to Georg Spalatin (1484–1545), secretary to Elector Frederick "the Wise" (1463–1525) of Saxony, asking Spalatin, a learned humanist, to join this endeavor, specifically by "adapt[ing] any one of the psalms for use as a hymn . . . ."[18] Luther wrote to Spalatin of his plan "to compose psalms for the people [in the] vernacular, that is, spiritual songs, so that the Word of God may be among the people also in the form of music."[19] Once again,

12

Luther made clear that music is for proclaiming the Word of God ("that the Word of God may be among the people also in the form of music").

In a 1530 letter to the composer Ludwig Senfl (ca. 1486 – between December 2, 1542, and August 10, 1543), Luther again praised music: "except for theology there is no art that could be put on the same level with music . . . ."[20] A few lines later he wrote of the Old Testament prophets: "They held theology and music most tightly connected, and proclaimed truth through Psalms and songs."[21] For Luther, theology and music were to be "tightly connected," and music ["Psalms and songs"] was to "proclaim truth."

Those two nuggets from Luther's writings are valuable guiding principles for the twenty-first-century Lutheran church musician. In our music-making, theology and music should always be "tightly connected." That proposition has to do with our musical choices – as much as possible we should choose hymns, choral and vocal music, and instrumental music that can be "tightly connected" to the theology of each day in the church year, that is, by relating musical choices as much as possible to the specified lectionary readings for each Sunday and feast day in the church year. When we proceed in that way music will have the potential to "proclaim truth." We should expect nothing less in our work as Lutheran church musicians.

One final quotation from Luther, the shortest of all those cited here, comes from his Table Talk. Recorded sometime before December 14, 1531, by Johann Schlaginhaufen, Luther said: "God has preached the gospel through music too, as may be seen in Josquin . . . ."[22] Choosing the preeminent composer of his day, Josquin des Prez (ca. 1450/55–1521), Luther again emphasized that the Gospel is proclaimed through music. For Luther this was the high purpose of music in worship.

What Does Luther's Thought Imply?

In his Small Catechism, Luther consistently posed the question "Was ist das?" ("What is this?"). Our English-language translations today more frequently preface Luther's catechetical explanations with the question "What does this mean?" That same question might be posed here – given Luther's thought on the purpose of music in worship, what does this mean for us as twenty-first-century Lutheran church musicians?

Luther's high purpose for music in worship provides meaning, significance, and focus for our work as twenty-first-century Lutheran church musicians. It also imposes an obligation, namely that in our musical choices, be they congregational hymns, vocal and choral music, or instrumental music, we never settle merely for presenting musical objects, no matter their aesthetic beauty. Luther's purpose for music – music as proclamation of the Word of God – helps us to determine the *why* of our musical choices. Why do we choose a particular hymn, an organ setting of a hymn tune, or a choral motet? The music is chosen because it is "tightly connected" to theological emphases for the day or the season. In this way the music has the potential to repeat, support, and emphasize the Word of God, to *proclaim* the Word of God. Luther's view of the high purpose of music in worship helps us to see the weakness of choosing the merely aesthetic as well as the trivial and banal, to understand that music of perhaps great beauty might, nonetheless, be irrelevant to the proclamation of the Word of God, to perceive that music connected to the pop culture of the day is a poor match for "the depth of the riches and wisdom and knowledge of God" (Rom 11:33).

Michael Praetorius (1571–1621) on the Purpose of Music in Worship

Michael Praetorius was one of the most prolific of early Lutheran composers, his numerous settings of Lutheran chorales filling some nineteen large volumes of the modern collected edition of his works.[23] In addition to being a prolific composer, Praetorius took an encyclopedic approach to writing about music; his *Syntagma Musicum* was planned as four volumes, of which the first three appeared between 1615 and 1619. The first volume (1615), written in Latin and intended primarily for the Lutheran clergy, focused on the sacred music of the church. The second volume (1618) dealt with instruments (including a substantial treatment of the organ), while the third volume (1619) focused on musical forms, aspects of music theory and notation, and matters of performance practice. Volumes two and three, intended for musicians, were written in German. The proposed fourth volume, treating music composition, was apparently never completed and did not appear prior to Praetorius's death in 1621.

Praetorius's father, also named Michael, worked with Johann Walter, Luther's musical advisor and collaborator, at the Torgau Latin school, where the younger Michael studied music with Michael Voigt, who succeeded Walter as cantor. Thus, Praetorius had a direct link—through his father—to Walter, and ultimately to Luther. In *Syntagma Musicum I*, Praetorius referred to Walter as "the solemn and melodious founder of Lutheran music."[24] With this very close connection to Walter and Luther, it is not surprising to see Praetorius define a purpose for music that is closely related to Luther's foundational writings.

Already in the second paragraph of *Syntagma Musicum I*, Praetorius linked music with preaching, song with sermon, by incorporating a clever little play on words—juxtaposing the similar-sounding Latin words *concio* and *cantio*.[25] A *concio* is literally a speech made in the context of a public assembly; Praetorius used the word to refer to the pastor's sermon in a Lutheran service. A *cantio* is a song; Praetorius used the word to refer to the sacred music of the church sung within the Divine Service (*Gottesdienst*), as well as in the Offices of Matins and Vespers—thus, German-language chorales and also Latin sacred music, which, thanks to Luther's favorable attitudes toward Latin chant and polyphony, continued to find a prominent place in Lutheran liturgies. In his opening "Dedicatory Epistle" to *Syntagma Musicum I*, Praetorius wrote:

> . . . two occupations are required for the complete and finished perfection of the divine liturgy, as it is carried out at the public gatherings of the church, namely, speech and song.[26] [*Concionem* and *Cantionem*; sermon and song]

A few pages later he restated that theme:

> . . . so should those entrusted with the supervision of the church completely avoid ever separating or pulling apart speech and song [*Concio* and *Cantio*] in . . . the public liturgy. . . . so does the perfect and complete liturgy consist of two duties, that is, speech and song.[27] [*concionandi* and *cantandi*; preaching and making music]

While Luther would state that theology and music were to be "tightly connected," Praetorius would write that concio and cantio should never be separated or pulled apart. Clearly, both Luther and Praetorius articulated the same position.

A few pages later, Praetorius is more specific about the shared content of concio and cantio:

> . . . speech and song preach and celebrate the doctrine of the same confession of Christ and of the propitiation made by his blood. . . .[28]

Of particular importance here are two things: 1) Praetorius asserts that song (i.e., music) *preaches*, and 2) that both speech and song preach *Christ*. Thus, in Praetorius's view, there is not only a shared *purpose* but also a shared Christological *content* between the sermon and the music of the Divine Service. In his 1619 collection of chorale settings, the *Polyhymnia Caduceatrix et Panegyrica*, Praetorius repeated this principle, first stated four years earlier in *Syntagma Musicum I*:

> . . . for the completeness of worship, it is not only appropriate to have a *Concio*, a good sermon, but also in addition the necessary *Cantio*, good music and song.[29]

What Does Praetorius's Premise Imply?

What is the significance of the concio/cantio principle articulated by Praetorius? What does it mean with respect to the *purpose* of music in Lutheran worship? By stating this premise in 1615, and by repeating it in

1619, Praetorius asserted a fundamental principle of Lutheran church music, established by Luther and still a bedrock proposition for Lutheran music-making, namely that *preaching and music operate on the same plane and strive for the same goal—both proclaim the Word of God*. This principle elevates music to a very high purpose indeed—like Lutheran sermons (concio), Lutheran music (cantio) is to preach and proclaim the good news of salvation and eternal life in Christ. Precisely *how* Praetorius did this in his own music—in his own *practice*—will be explored in the next chapter. Suffice it to say here that Praetorius shared with Luther a high purpose for music in Lutheran worship, founded on a tight, even seamless, connection between theology and music.

Heinrich Schütz (1585–1672) and the Purpose of Music in Worship

Unlike Praetorius, Heinrich Schütz was not inclined toward voluminous prose writings about music. Surviving letters and documents show Schütz tending to practical administrative matters, such as payment of salaries for his court musicians.[30] Thus, unlike Luther and Praetorius, Schütz did not write about, much less define, the purpose of music in worship. We will see in Chapter Two that, in fact, his music proclaims the Word of God, and does so brilliantly. There is, however, one document—the sermon preached at Schütz's funeral, by the Saxon court preacher Martin Geier—that provides a clue regarding how Schütz himself might have understood the purpose of music in worship. Robin A. Leaver characterized this sermon as one that:

> . . . presents a Lutheran view of the place of music in Christian life and worship. In other words, it presents the theological presuppositions that conditioned the climate within which Schütz worked.[31]

Thus, while we lack Schütz's own thoughts on the purpose of music in worship, Geier's sermon, it is fair to say, reflects the theological framework within which Schütz composed music that proclaimed the Word of God. One excerpt from Geier's sermon will suffice here:

> We, for our part, finally take home with us the teaching that making songs, singing songs, accompanying songs with musical instruments cannot by any means be displeasing to God the Lord, but rather that the Holy Spirit Himself always makes His influence felt herein, yes, that public worship itself has always, by divine command, been provided with such music.[32]

Here, Geier sounds very much like Luther in the 1538 preface to Rhau's *Symphoniae Iucundae*: "The Holy Ghost himself honors her [i.e., music] as an instrument for his proper work" (cf. note 13). Geier, in effect, summarized the theological/musical premise under which Schütz composed his music of Gospel proclamation.

Johann Sebastian Bach (1685–1750) and the Purpose of Music in Worship

Like Schütz, his illustrious forebear in the Lutheran cantorate, Johann Sebastian Bach did not write reflectively about music. Bach's writings, collected in the first volume of the series Bach-Dokumente,[33]and presented selectively in English translation in *The New Bach Reader*,[34] tend to focus on practical matters relating to, for example, his own employment (obtaining new positions, being released from previous positions, seeking potential new opportunities), assisting others to obtain new positions by writing letters of recommendation, providing evaluations of organs that he tested and inspected, and writing to church or town officials seeking their support for an adequate number of qualified musicians. Bach did not write about or define his views on the purpose of music in worship.[35] We are not, however, without significant clues that reveal how Bach worked as a church musician, how he perceived the integration of music in the Divine Service.

On September 20, 1728, Bach wrote to the Leipzig town council to complain that the subdeacon at the St. Nicholas Church, Gottlieb Gaudlitz, had begun to usurp Bach's duties of hymn selection. The interesting detail in this letter is Bach's statement of methodology regarding his practice of hymn selection:

> . . . on the occasion of my acceptance of the call to the Cantorate of the St. Thomas School here [in Leipzig], which is entrusted to me, I was instructed . . . to abide in all things strictly by the customs hitherto followed at the public divine service, and not to make any innovations . . . . Among these customs and practices was the ordering of the hymns before and after the sermons, which was always left solely to me and my predecessors in the Cantorate to determine, in accordance with the gospels and the *Dresdener Gesangbuch* [the Dresden hymnal used at that point in Leipzig churches] based on the same, as seemed appropriate to the season . . . .[36]

In this letter of protest, Bach attests to his own procedures in working toward that ideal described by Luther in his 1530 letter to Senfl, namely that "theology and music [should be] most tightly connected." Bach's goal was to choose hymns "in accordance with the gospels" and "appropriate to the season," i.e., the church year. Thus, while Bach does not write explicitly about the purpose of music in worship, this detail from his 1728 letter demonstrates his desire for a purposeful integration (a tight connection) of hymns with: 1) the Gospel lesson (as specified by the lectionary), 2) the sermon (normally an explication of the Gospel lesson for the day), and 3) the church year.

Moreover, the custom in Leipzig to position a cantata between the reading of the Gospel lesson and the preaching of the sermon,[37] meant that normal practice provided for both a musical exposition of the Gospel (i.e., the cantata) and a spoken (preached) exposition of that same Gospel (i.e., the sermon). Thus, when he came to Leipzig in 1723, Bach inherited a situation that required music to be proclamation of the Gospel. Particularly in his cantatas, but also in his organ chorale preludes,[38] Bach provided music that was tightly connected to the theological focus of the day, music that proclaimed the Word of God. With respect to precisely *how* Bach accomplished that task, in the next chapter we will examine an excerpt from a cantata and an organ chorale prelude as examples of Bach's practice of music as proclamation.

Summary

This chapter has focused on the *purpose* of Lutheran church music — as proclamation of the Gospel, of the Word of God. It was Martin Luther who wrote time and again that the purpose of music is to proclaim God's Word, that music is to be "tightly connected" to theology, that music is to "proclaim truth." Michael Praetorius, one of the greatest of Lutheran composers, reiterated Luther's thought early in the seventeenth century. His premise, that sermon and music (concio and cantio) exist on the same plane and for the same purpose — to proclaim the Word of God — brought Luther's views on the purpose of church music into the early seventeenth century. Praetorius's illustrious heirs as Lutheran cantors — Heinrich Schütz and Johann Sebastian Bach — did not articulate in prose the purpose of Lutheran church music, the *why* of Lutheran church music, though their careers provide clues regarding the presuppositions that would have been guiding principles for their work as Lutheran cantors. It is the music itself of Schütz and Bach that illustrates with clarity their desire to proclaim the Word of God through music. In the next chapter we will examine music by Schütz and Bach to help us understand *how* music proclaims the Word of God.

Notes

1 Tim Wright, *A Community of Joy: How to Create Contemporary Worship*, Effective Church Series (Nashville: Abingdon Press, 1994), 22.

2 Terri Bocklund McLean, *New Harmonies: Choosing Contemporary Music for Worship* (Bethesda, Md.: Alban Institute, 1998), 30.

3 Arthur A. Just Jr., *Heaven on Earth: The Gifts of Christ in the Divine Service* (St. Louis: Concordia Publishing House, 2008), 16.

4 A now classic statement on this topic is Norman Nagel's "Introduction" to *Lutheran Worship* (St. Louis: Concordia Publishing House, 1982), 6–7.

5 Michael David Fleming, "Michael Praetorius, Music Historian: An Annotated Translation of *Syntagma Musicum* I, Part I" (PhD diss., Washington University, 1979), 110. This source is subsequently cited as: Praetorius, *Syntagma Musicum I.*

6 Oswald Bayer, *Living by Faith: Justification and Sanctification*, trans. Geoffrey W. Bromiley (Grand Rapids, Mich.: Eerdmans, 2003), 53, 56. Bayer also treats Luther's hymn "Dear Christians, One and All, Rejoice" in his book *Martin Luther's Theology: A Contemporary Interpretation*, trans. Thomas H. Trapp (Grand Rapids, Mich.: Eerdmans, 2008), 214–24.

7 Martin Luther, *Liturgy and Hymns*, ed. Ulrich S. Leupold, Luther's Works, vol. 53 (Philadelphia: Fortress Press, 1965), 323–24. This volume is subsequently cited as: LW 53.

8 For further discussion of this point, see Roger D. Pittelko, "Worship and the Community of Faith," in *Lutheran Worship: History and Practice*, ed. Fred L. Precht (St. Louis: Concordia Publishing House, 1993), 44–57.

9 1 Cor 2:14: "The natural person does not accept the things of the Spirit of God, for they are folly to him, and he is not able to understand them because they are spiritually discerned."

10 John W. Kleinig, "What's the Use of Praising God?" *Lutheran Theological Journal* 38/2 (2004): 84.

11 LW 53, 321.

12 LW 53, 323.

13 Ibid.

14 Kolb/Wengert, SC 355–56.

15 LW 53, 316.

16 Ibid.

17 Ibid., 333.

18 Martin Luther, *Letters II*, ed. Gottfried G. Krodel, Luther's Works, vol. 49 (Philadelphia: Fortress Press, 1972), 69. This volume is subsequently cited as LW 49.

19 LW 49, 68.

20 LW 49, 428.

21 Ibid.

22 Martin Luther, *Table Talk*, ed. Theodore G. Tappert, Luther's Works, vol. 54 (Philadelphia: Fortress Press, 1967), 129–30. This volume is subsequently cited as LW 54.

23 *Gesamtausgabe der musikalischen Werke von Michael Praetorius*, ed. Friedrich Blume, 20 vols. (Wolfenbüttel: Kallmeyer, 1928–1956).

24 *Syntagma Musicum I*, 60. In this treatise Praetorius also included a separate section on Walter, with a lengthy quotation from Walter himself; see pages 308–16 of Fleming's translation.

25 I am indebted to Robin Leaver for first drawing my attention to "concio et cantio."

26 *Syntagma Musicum I*, 4.

27 Ibid., 7.

28 Ibid., 10.

29 Quoted in Robin A. Leaver, *Luther's Liturgical Music: Principles and Implications*, Lutheran Quarterly Books (Grand Rapids, Mich.: Eerdmans, 2007), 287.

30 Gina Spagnoli, *Letters and Documents of Heinrich Schütz 1656–1672: An Annotated Translation* (Ann Arbor: UMI Research Press, 1990).

31 Robin A. Leaver, *Music in the Service of the Church: The Funeral Sermon for Heinrich Schütz (1585–1672)*, Church Music Pamphlet Series (St. Louis: Concordia Publishing House, 1984), 8.

32 Ibid., 36.

33 *Schriftstücke von der Hand Johann Sebastian Bachs: Kritische Gesamtausgabe*, ed. Werner Neumann and Hans-Joachim Schulze, Bach-Dokumente, 1 (Kassel: Bärenreiter, 1963).

34 *The New Bach Reader: A Life of Johann Sebastian Bach in Letters and Documents*, rev. and enl. Christoph Wolff (New York: W. W. Norton, 1998).

35 Bach's 1730 memorandum to the Leipzig Town Council, entitled "Short But Most Necessary Draft for a Well-Appointed Church Music, with Certain Modest Reflections on the Decline of the Same" is not, as the title might imply, a kind of position paper on what constitutes good church music. Rather, it is Bach's plea for a sufficient number of well-qualified musicians to fulfill his duties in providing music for the Leipzig churches. Similarly, in the 1708 letter requesting release from his position as organist at the St. Blasius church in Mühlhausen, Bach mentions his goal of "a well-regulated [*regulirte*] church music, to the Glory of God" but without defining even minimally what might be implied by "well-regulated."

36 *The New Bach Reader*, 137–38.

37 Ibid., 113. See document no. 113, Bach's handwritten outline for the "Order of the Divine Service in Leipzig," probably for November 28, 1723, the First Sunday in Advent that year.

38 Ibid., 113. In the order of service for Advent 1, Bach specified during the distribution of Holy Communion: "alternate preluding and singing of chorales until the end of the Communion." Since the distribution of Holy Communion at either of Leipzig's principal churches, St. Thomas or St. Nicholas, typically occupied the last third of a three-hour Sunday morning service, there was the potential for playing several organ chorale preludes as introductions to the sung chorales.

2

THE PRACTICE OF LUTHERAN CHURCH MUSIC

Having seen in the writings of Luther and Praetorius the premise that church music was intended to participate in the task of proclaiming the Word of God, thus having established the *why* of Lutheran church music, the logical next question is to ask *how* music might proclaim the Word of God. *How* does music have the ability to "proclaim truth," as Luther would have it? In this chapter we explore the practice of Lutheran church music as proclamation. Once again we will turn to Luther, Praetorius, Schütz, and Bach as case studies, and with Schütz and Bach we will examine specific compositions to understand how music proclaims the Word of God. Along the way, we will also explore the concepts that music has meaning and that music expresses identity. It is worth emphasizing again that Luther, Praetorius, Schütz, and Bach have something to teach us historically in the way of guiding principles for the practice of Lutheran church music. Thus, the point here is not that twenty-first-century Lutheran church musicians should draw solely or even principally on these historic repertoires, but rather that we should learn from these composers and repertoires how Lutheran church music — whether old or new, simple or complex — might proclaim the Word of God.

Luther Sets the Tone

Luther defined the purpose of music in worship: to proclaim the Word of God. Simultaneously, he established guiding principles for the *practice* of Lutheran church music — principles that continue to be relevant in our own time. He did so in four distinct but interrelated ways: 1) by retaining rather than discarding the church's heritage of sacred music; 2) by creating a rich body of vernacular hymnody for the people to sing — in schools and homes as well as in church; 3) by valuing the craft of musical composition—by the finest composers of sacred polyphonic music of his day; 4) by discerning that music from the popular culture was not a good choice for use within the church.

Retaining the Church's Musical Heritage

Luther was not inclined to discard the musical heritage of the church. In an early pronouncement in his 1523 *Von ordenung gottis diensts ynn der gemeyne* ("Concerning the Order of Public Worship"), Luther wrote: "Let the chants in the Sunday masses and Vespers be retained; they are quite good and are taken from Scripture."[1]

In that same year his more detailed statement on the Mass appeared in print: the *Formula Missae et Communionis pro Ecclesia Vuittembergensi* ("An Order of Mass and Communion for the Church at Wittenberg").[2] While Luther was reluctant to imply that the manner in which the Latin Mass was celebrated in Wittenberg should be seen as somehow normative, he acquiesced in publishing an order of the Latin Mass simply because so many were seeking his guidance on this important matter, as they began to implement reforms in their own towns and churches. In the *Formula Missae* he made clear that he wished to retain most of the liturgical and musical heritage of the Mass. As he had written earlier in 1523, "Let the chants . . . be retained," so also in the *Formula Missae* he advocated retaining the church's rich heritage of Latin chant:

> First, we approve and retain the introits for the Lord's days and the festivals of Christ, such as Easter, Pentecost, and the Nativity . . . .[3]

> Second, we accept the Kyrie eleison in the form in which it has been used until now, with the various melodies for different seasons, together with the Angelic Hymn, Gloria in Excelsis . . . .[4]

Note that Luther referred specifically to retaining the music ("the various melodies") that was already in use in the church.

> Fourth, the gradual of two verses shall be sung, either together with the Alleluia, or one of the two, as the bishop [pastor] may decide.[5]

> Seventh, the custom of singing the Nicene Creed does not displease us . . . .[6]

Thus, as in the brief "Concerning the Order of Public Worship," so also in the more detailed *Formula Missae*, Luther showed that he valued the heritage of Latin chant and wished to retain this music in the worship practice at Wittenberg. He repeated this point later in his career; recorded in the Table Talk (June 25, 1539) is this statement from Luther: "It would be good to keep the whole liturgy with its music, omitting only the canon."[7] In the *Formula Missae* Luther pronounced the Canon of the Mass "that abominable concoction drawn from everyone's sewer and cesspool. The mass became a sacrifice."[8] He labeled the Offertory "that utter abomination . . . . From here on almost everything smacks and savors of sacrifice."[9] Thus, Luther made no provision in the *Formula Missae* for the Offertory chants, since that part of the Mass was completely unacceptable on theological grounds — emphasizing an incorrect sacrificial understanding of the Mass. But apart from the Offertory, Luther wished to retain all other monophonic chant from the inherited tradition of the Latin Mass.

Creating Vernacular Hymnody

As much as Luther wished to retain the treasure of Latin chant that had long been such an important part of the Western Christian tradition, he was eager as well to have the people sing in their own language. Cited in the previous chapter was Luther's 1523 letter to Spalatin, where he sought Spalatin's assistance in his plan "to compose psalms for the people [in the] vernacular, that is, spiritual songs, so that the Word of God may be among the people also in the form of music."[10] The task of creating a repertory of German-language hymns was very much on Luther's mind in 1523; he also expressed this desire toward the end of his *Formula Missae*:

> I also wish that we had as many songs as possible in the vernacular which the people could sing during mass, immediately after the gradual and also after the Sanctus and Agnus Dei. For who doubts that originally all the people sang these which now only the choir sings or responds to while the bishop [i.e., pastor] is consecrating? The bishops may have these [congregational] hymns sung either after the Latin chants, or use the Latin on one [Sun]day and the vernacular on the next, until the time comes that the whole mass is sung in the vernacular. But poets are wanting among us, or not yet known, who could compose evangelical and spiritual songs, as Paul calls them [Col. 3:16], worthy to be used in the church of God.[11]

Luther wanted the people to sing the Gospel in hymns written in their own language. While he looked forward to the day when the entire Mass could be sung in the vernacular, he was perfectly happy to mix Latin chant and vernacular hymns in a Sunday service, or to alternate Latin and German from one Sunday to the next.[12] Thus, he was pragmatic in terms of introducing vernacular psalms and hymns. But he was also insistent that the new German-language hymns had to be "worthy to be used in the church of God." Indeed he closed that paragraph of the *Formula Missae* by stating that "few [hymns] are found that are written in a proper devotional style. I mention this to encourage any German poets to compose evangelical hymns for us."[13] Hence the 1523 letter to Spalatin, where Luther offered advice about the literary style he wished to see in this new repertory of vernacular hymns (in this instance he refers specifically to a translation into German of a psalm):

> But I would like you to avoid any new words or the language used at court. In order to be understood by the people, only the simplest and the most common words should be used for singing; at the same time, however, they should be pure and apt; and further, the sense should be clear and as close as possible to the psalm.[14]

Luther's criteria for hymns—"worthy to be used in the church of God" and "in a proper devotional style"—are important to note, for these comments demonstrate his conviction that the creation of a repertory, in both its textual and musical dimensions, had to be judged with regard to quality; not just any poetic or musical expression would suffice.

Luther must have been working feverishly during 1523–1524 to create this new repertory of vernacular hymns, for the first printed collections of German-language hymns (or *chorales*) appeared in 1524. *Etlich Cristlich lider* (Nuremberg, 1524), the so-called "Achtliederbuch," included eight hymns, four by Luther.[15] The very first hymn in that collection is Luther's magnificent hymn of Law and Gospel, "Nun freut euch, lieben Christen g'mein" ("Dear Christians, One and All, Rejoice").[16] Immediately following is the equally rich hymn by Paul Speratus, "Es ist das Heil uns kommen her" ("Salvation unto Us Has Come").[17] For each of these hymns the printer included musical notation for the melody, followed by the hymn stanzas. Consistent with the proclamatory nature of the early Reformation chorale, each stanza of Speratus's hymn is preceded by an alphabet letter as a reference key (fourteen stanzas labeled from "a" to "o", see ex. 1), and on the two pages following the hymn one finds citations of multiple scriptural passages that bear on each stanza of the poetry (ex. 2), thus demonstrating clearly that this hymn was conceived as sung proclamation of the Word of God.[18] Two hymnals published in Erfurt in 1524, each entitled "Enchiridion," provided twenty-six German-language hymns—an impressive number

ℂWas ich gethan haß vnd gelert/Das soltu thůn vñ leren/
Damit das Reich Gottes werdt gemert/Zu loß vnd seinen
eren/Vnd hůt dich für menschen satz/Daruon verdirbt der
edle schatz. Das laß ich dir zur letze.

1 5 2 3   Mart. Luth.

Ein lied vom gesetz vnd glauben/gewal-
tigklich mit götlicher schrifft verlegt.
Doctoris Pauli Sperati.

Es ist das hayl vns kumen her.

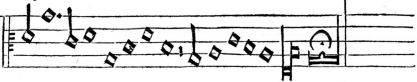

A   Es ist das hayl vns kumen her/Von gnad vnnd lauter
gůten/Die werck helffen nymmer mer/Sie mügen nicht Be-
hüten/Der glauß sihet Jesum Christum an/Der hat gnug
für vns alle gethan/Er ist der mitler worden.

B Was Got im gesetz gebotten hat/Do man es nicht kondt
halten/Erhůß sich zorn vnd grosse not/Für Got so manig-
falte/Vom fleysch wolt nicht herauß der geyst/Vom gesetz
erfordert aller meyst/Es war mit vns vorloren.

Example 1. "Es ist das Heil uns kommen her," *Etlich Cristlich lider*
(Nuremberg, 1524)

Anzaygung auß der schrifft warauff diß
gesang allenthalben ist gegründet/Darauff sich alle
vnser sach verlassen mag.

A→ **A** Ephe.2.Das er anzaygt die vberschwenckliche reichthumb seiner gnaden/in freündtligkait.

Ro.3. Kain fleysch durch des gesetz werck für jm mag rechtfertig sein.

Ebre.12.Wir auffsehen auff den Hertzogen vnsers glaubens/vnd auff den volender Jesum.

Ebre.2.Der durch die gnade gottes für alle versucht hat den todt.

Ebre.9.Vnd darumb ist er auch ein mitler des newen Testaments.

B→ **B** Ro.8.Dem gesetz gottes ist das fleisch nit vnterthan/es mags auch nit.

Ro.4.Seyntemal das gesetz richt nur zorn an.

Ro.7.Wir wissen/das das gesetz geystlich ist/aber ich bin fleyschlich.

Johannis.16. On mich mügt jr nichts thun.

Galath.3.Die schrifft hats alles beschlossen vnder der sünde/auff das die verhaissung keme durch den glauben an Christum.

C→ **C** Als oben Rom.8. Dem gesetz gottes ist kain fleysch vnderthan/es vermags auch nit.

Rom.3.Durch das gesetz kumbt die erkantnuß der sünde.

Rom.7. Ich wüste nit das die lust sünde wer/so nit saget das gesetz. Laß dich nichts gelusten.

D Eph.2.Wir waren auch kinder des zorns von natur.

Rom.7.Das gesetz ist neben einkummen/das die sünde ye grösser wurde.

Matth.23. Wee euch jr gleyßner/zu dem achtenden mal.

Psal.50.Sihe in boßhait bin ich empfangen/vnd in sünden geborn.

E Matth.5. Nicht ein spitzlin noch ein buchstaben sol vndergeen/es muß alles geschehen.

Ebre.1.Er hat sein sun geschickt/das er die vnter dem gesetz waren/erlöset.

Rom.8.Er hat verdampt die sünde im fleysch durch sünde/das die gerechtigkait des gesetz in vns erfüllet wurde.

Rom.1. Der zorn gottes wirt offenbar/vber alles gotloß wesen.

F Rom.7.Aber yetzt seind wir ledig worden von dem gesetz des todts.

Rom.12.Verendert euch in vernewerung ewers syns/das jr prüfft den willen gottes.

Johannis.11. Ich bin die aufferstehung vnd das leben/Wer in mich glaubt der wirt leben ob er gleich sturbe.

Evidence from the Scriptures on which this
hymn is in all respects grounded / Thereupon all
our concerns may rely.

A [= stanza 1 of "Es ist das Heil uns kommen her"]

Ephesians 2 [:7]
Romans 3 [:20a]
Hebrews 12 [:2a]
Hebrews 2 [:9c]
Hebrews 9 [:15a]

B [= stanza 2 of "Es ist das Heil uns kommen her"]

Romans 8 [:7b]
Romans 4 [:15a]
Romans 7 [:14]
John [15:5c]
Galatians 3 [:22]

C [=stanza 3 of "Es ist das Heil uns kommen her"]

Romans 8 [:7b]
Romans 3 [:20b]
Romans 7 [:7c]

. . . and so on through all fourteen stanzas of the hymn

Example 2. *On the opposite page,* scriptural basis for each stanza of "Es ist das
Heil uns kommen her," *Etlich Cristlich lider* (Nuremberg, 1524); *on this page,*
as an example, lists of the scriptural passages cited for the first three stanzas.

for this newly emerging genre.[19] Also appearing in 1524 was a significant collection of polyphonic settings of these new German-language hymns, the settings composed by Luther's colleague, Johann Walter. His *Geystliche gesangk Buchleyn* (Wittenberg, 1524) included four- and five-part settings of thirty-two hymns, twenty-four of them by Luther.[20]

Given this amazing creation of a new repertory of vernacular hymns in a quite brief period of time, it would be only natural to imagine congregations in Wittenberg and elsewhere in the mid-1520s actively singing the Word of God. But congregational singing was not an easy or automatic proposition, given a society that was only partially literate and church practice that had not previously encouraged regular use of congregational song. That the people did not take quickly to singing in church caused Luther some frustration. Joseph Herl has translated excerpts from sermons of 1526 and 1529 in which Luther criticized the people in Wittenberg for not singing the German hymns that he (and others) had written, the intent being that these texts and melodies would play an integral role in the Christian formation of the people.[21]

Two years after this flurry of chorale publication, Luther's *Deutsche Messe* was published in 1526. In his preface, Luther made clear that he did not want to "discontinue the service in the Latin language," stressing the value of language study for the young,[22] but he prepared a German Mass "for the sake of the unlearned lay folk."[23] Vernacular hymns were specified by Luther at various points in the *Deutsche Messe*:

> To begin the service we sing a hymn or a German Psalm in the First Tone . . . .[24]

> After the Epistle a German hymn, either "Now Let Us Pray to the Holy Ghost" ["Nun bitten wir den Heiligen Geist"] or any other, is sung with the whole choir ["und das mit dem ganzen Chor"].[25]

> After the Gospel the whole congregation sings the Creed in German: "In One True God We All Believe" ["Wir glauben all an einen Gott"].[26]

During the distribution of the Lord's Supper Luther recommended the singing of additional hymns:

> Meanwhile, the German Sanctus ["Jesaia, dem Propheten, das geschah"] or the hymn, "Let God Be Blest" ["Gott sei gelobet und gebenedeiet"], or the hymn of John Huss, "Jesus Christ, Our God and Savior" ["Jesus Christus, unser Heiland, der von uns"], could be sung. Then shall the cup be blessed and administered, while

the remainder of these hymns are sung, or the German Agnus Dei ["Christe, du Lamm Gottes"].[27]

Thus, Luther identified specific places for vernacular hymns in his *Deutsche Messe*, by this means providing the possibility of musical proclamation through hymns.[28] Luther added the following disclaimer near the end of the *Deutsche Messe*:

> But on the festivals, such as Christmas, Easter, Pentecost, St. Michael's, Purification, and the like, we must continue to use Latin until we have enough German songs. This work is just beginning; not everything has been prepared that is needed.[29]

While Luther continued to assert the value of singing Latin texts in both the *Formula Missae* and the *Deutsche Messe*, his energetic creation of the repertory of German-language hymns provided an important means of sung proclamation in the Mass, as well as a pedagogical and catechetical help in schools and homes.[30]

Valuing the Craft of Polyphonic Sacred Music

In addition to retaining the church's musical heritage of Latin chant, Luther, who loved music, was eager to see the best sacred polyphonic music used in the church to proclaim the Word of God. In his 1538 preface to Rhau's *Symphoniae Iucundae*, Luther wrote with a sense of wonder concerning the intricacies of sixteenth-century polyphony. Referring to "God's absolute and perfect wisdom in his wondrous work of music," he observed:

> Here it is most remarkable that one single voice continues to sing the tenor [i.e., the cantus firmus or preexistent melody], while at the same time many other voices play around it, exulting and adorning it in exuberant strains and, as it were, leading it forth in a divine roundelay, so that those who are the least bit moved know nothing more amazing in this world.[31]

Luther knew the music of the best composers of his time. In the Table Talk, Luther referred specifically to Josquin, arguably the finest composer of the early sixteenth century:

> God has preached the Gospel through music, too, as may be seen in the songs of Josquin, all of whose compositions flow freely, gently, and cheerfully, are not forced or cramped by rules like the song of the finch.[32]

And when Luther desired a polyphonic setting of a particular chant antiphon, he requested it from no less a composer than Ludwig Senfl.[33] By 1523 Senfl was serving as composer at the Munich court chapel of Duke Wilhelm IV of Bavaria, having served previously in Emperor Maximilian I's court chapel in Vienna until the emperor's death in 1519 and the dissolution of the imperial chapel in 1520. That Luther was well acquainted with the best art music of his time—and that he had a great love for this music—is clear from his reference to Josquin and his correspondence with Senfl. Further, we have the testimony of Johann Walter, as recorded by Michael Praetorius in volume one of *Syntagma Musicum*, where Walter observed:

> I know and bear true witness that the holy man of God, Luther, who has been Prophet and Apostle to the German nations, had a great love for music in plainsong and polyphony. I have sung for many precious hours with him, and often seen how the dear man became so merry and joyful in spirit from singing, that he could hardly become tired and weary of singing and of speaking so splendidly about music.[34]

Avoiding the Use of Popular Music in the Church

One of the most persistent myths about Luther is that he brought the popular music of his day into the church. It is not uncommon to read assertions such as: "Martin Luther, for example, was no stranger to entertainment. He took tunes that were sung in bars and wrote God-inspired words to go along with the melodies," though the author of that assertion provided no examples of such melodies or texts.[35] Another author wrote: "The tune of Martin Luther's 'A Mighty Fortress Is Our God' is borrowed from a popular song of his day," an assertion that the author is unable to substantiate by pointing to a specific popular song of Luther's day or to a source for that song.[36] Other writers have asserted a Luther who reportedly mused "Why should the devil have all the good tunes?" But searching Luther's works has turned up no such quotation; indeed, standard reference sources attribute that line to the Rev. Rowland Hill (1744–1833), an English clergyman.[37] While advocates for the use of pop music in the late twentieth- and twenty-first-century church have tried to enlist Luther as an ally, the truth will not permit it.

The case of his hymn "From Heaven Above to Earth I Come" is instructive in this regard. While Luther originally coupled this tune with an existing popular song, "Ich komm aus frembden Landen her," he eventually wrote a new tune (the one we sing today) as this hymn was included in printed hymnals and became available to the wider church, e.g., through the 1545 *Geystliche Lieder* (Leipzig: Valentin Babst), the well-known "Babst

Gesangbuch."[38] With his provision of a newly composed tune for his Christmas hymn, we see Luther very consciously *not* borrowing from the popular culture of his time when he had the opportunity to do precisely that, had he found it desirable to do so.

In his preface to Walter's 1524 choral hymnal, Luther referred to the popular music of his time in this way:

> And these songs were arranged in four parts to give the young—who should at any rate be trained in music and other fine arts—something to wean them away from love ballads and carnal songs and to teach them something of value in their place . . . .[39]

These are clearly not the words of one who would embrace the popular music of his day for use in the church. Thus, twentieth- and twenty-first-century writers who seek Luther's blessing for the use of popular music in church are turning to the wrong figure.[40] One simply cannot construe Luther's musical procedures or written statements as lending support to the practice of using music from the popular culture in the church's worship.

Luther's Principles of Music Practice—What Do They Mean?

Beyond the intrinsic value of understanding Luther's liturgical and musical attitudes and agenda, what does it mean for the twenty-first-century Lutheran church musician that Luther retained chant and polyphony, created a new repertory of German-language hymns, valued the finest art music of his day, and was discerning about not bringing the popular music of his time into the church? In what ways do Luther's views matter to the twenty-first-century Lutheran church musician? One can answer these questions on two levels, reflecting two chronological dimensions: 1) the accumulated heritage of music on which we continue to draw, and 2) current practice and the twenty-first-century debates on music in worship. First, Luther's love of music, his views on music, and his expectations concerning quality of music laid the foundation for five centuries of distinctly Lutheran composition—hymns, vocal and choral music, organ and other instrumental music. (Further, Luther's attitude toward the historic liturgy of the church provided a functional and meaningful role for these musical repertories.) Second, Luther's views on music offer critically important guiding principles for the debates on worship and music that continue into the twenty-first century.

Luther's retention of the Latin Mass with its chant, together with his retention of the Offices of Matins and Vespers, meant that the Lutheran church maintained a stable context for the practice of church music. His foundational work in creating an astonishingly rich repertory of German hymns led eventually to a strong tradition of congregational hymn singing.

His respect for the craft of musical composition required the Lutheran tradition to expect (and cultivate) skilled composers who could fashion music worthy of proclaiming the Word of God. Luther's love of polyphonic composition would be applied equally to Latin and German texts, the Latin motet tradition of the fifteenth and sixteenth centuries (e.g., Josquin and Senfl) being extended to the new genre of the German chorale (e.g., Walter's 1524 settings). Luther's attitudes laid the essential groundwork for subsequent generations of Lutheran composers and their repertories: the chorale settings of Praetorius, the Latin and German sacred music of Schütz, the cantatas and organ chorale settings of Bach, the choral settings of Lutheran chorales by Felix Mendelssohn (1809–1847), the Gospel motets of Jan Bender (1909–1994), the organ improvisations of Paul Manz (1919–2009), the hymn tunes and choral music of Carl Schalk (1929–), and the list goes on. All of those Lutheran repertories (and many more), with all the stylistic diversity of harmony, counterpoint, and rhythm that one would expect over the course of five centuries of music history, trace their functional origins to Luther's love for music and the guiding principles that he established. In short, these composers would not have created their rich repertories of congregational, vocal, and instrumental music were it not for Luther's views on music.

Luther's attitudes toward liturgy and music also speak to the debates about Lutheran worship and music that continue into the twenty-first century. That Luther did *not* reject the inherited liturgical traditions and musical repertories of his day could be a lesson for twenty-first-century Lutherans, some of whom have been much too quick to abandon their own traditions of liturgy and hymnody in favor of the worship and musical practices of American evangelicalism and pentecostalism. Luther did not abandon the historic liturgy, for he knew that in the *Gottesdienst*—God's Divine Service to His people—God delivers most fully His gifts of forgiveness, life, and salvation through His Word, through the water of Holy Baptism, and through the very body and blood of Jesus in His Holy Supper. Lutherans who willingly give up their liturgical and musical birthright argue that in so doing they will draw more people to the church by eliminating the "difficult barriers" that they suppose are inherent to Lutheran liturgy and music. But bringing people into a Lutheran church that chooses no longer to sing Lutheran theology, e.g., "Salvation unto us has come By God's free grace and favor," preferring instead to sing about our feelings toward God, is to deprive God's people of singing the Gospel, of proclaiming God's Word. Like Luther we should be eager to retain our inherited traditions of music — hymns for the people to sing the Gospel in church and at home, and well-crafted music of the highest quality, through which "God has preached the Gospel" — both in Luther's time and in our own time.

Like Luther we should also discern that popular music is a poor match for the task of proclaiming God's Word, of singing the Gospel. But precisely here we reach a central point of disagreement in the late twentieth- and twenty-first-century debates on worship and music in American Lutheranism.[41]

Popular Music in the Lutheran Church

Luther did not draw on the popular music of his time for use in the church. By contrast, today some would argue that popular music is exactly the way to attract more and more "unchurched" people to what might otherwise be for them the foreign experience of attending worship. The idea is to make "unchurched seekers" feel comfortable by providing for them in church the same musical sounds that they might listen to daily on radio stations or their own iPods. This proposition rests on a series of interrelated assumptions.

First, this proposition assumes that the purpose of music in Lutheran worship is to attract people to the church. But the purpose of music in Lutheran worship is to proclaim the Word of God (which is how Christians praise God), and it is the act of proclamation/praise in the Christian assembly that ultimately attracts people to the church, for the Holy Spirit works through that proclamation of the Word.

Second, this proposition assumes a predominantly homogeneous group of listeners who prefer the *popular* music of the average American radio station—not jazz, not classical, not folk music of whatever nationality, not bluegrass, and the list could go on. In fact, given myriad types of commercially available recorded music, one marvels at these presuppositions and the preference for a single style of popular music with roots planted squarely in the 1960s, i.e., hardly "contemporary" in the true sense of the word.

Third, the notion of drawing people to the church through popular music assumes that "unchurched seekers" want their experience with a church to be coupled with the same kind of (popular) music they supposedly encounter every day. Why do we assume that they would not prefer music that is uniquely of the church, music that takes them to a different place than the ubiquitous music of "adult contemporary" or "country" radio?

Fourth, bringing popular music into the church assumes that the Divine Service should be adjusted to suit uncatechized "seekers." In his essay "Orthodoxia, Orthopraxis, and Seekers," Frank Senn proposes an alternative point of view:

> Since the Christian worldview is nothing less than the new creation in Christ, our evangelism experts have proposed exactly the wrong strategy. We should not be deconstructing the liturgical orders that

celebrate and enact the new creation in order to accommodate the cultural expressions of the secular worldview; rather, through catechesis and ritual engagement we should be deconstructing the secular worldview within the seeker, who must "turn from idols to serve the living and true God" (I Thess. 1:9).[42]

It is not Senn's purpose to speak about how music is used within worship, but his idea of "deconstructing the secular worldview within the seeker" is incompatible with imitating pop musical styles in the church, in the hope that such music attracts the "seeker." Senn points out that the historic liturgy actually needs no adjustment to accommodate "seekers," since the reading and preaching of the Word of God has always been the focus of the first part (the "synaxis" or the "Mass of the Catechumens") of the historic Mass:

> What, then, do we do with seekers? We invite them into the life of God which is the church, the body of Christ on earth. Like the first two disciples who found the Messiah, we invite others to "come and see" Jesus (John 1:46). . . . Seekers should be invited to discover Christ himself in the church's age-old seeker service, the liturgy of the catechumens.[43]

Thus, we should attract the "unchurched seeker," *not* through pop musical styles but through the proclamation of the Word in the church's liturgy. The Holy Spirit works by means of that Word and, as it pleases Him, leads "seekers" to a deeper understanding through participation in the church's programs of catechesis.

Fifth, this proposition of using popular music to attract the "unchurched" assumes that drawing on the popular music of our culture is an action with no implications for the church, that music is somehow neutral, and that any kind of music can be used in the church. Rick Warren has stated this assumption succinctly: "Music is nothing more than an arrangement of notes and rhythms; it's the words that make a song spiritual."[44] If he is correct—that music is only an arrangement of pitches and rhythms—then it follows that music itself could actually play no role in proclamation, except as a neutral means to accommodate words. Further, it would mean that music is without any capacity for meaning and cannot signal identity. This issue has received little attention in the debates on music and worship and needs to be explored more fully here.

Music and Meaning

While Warren asserts that "Music is nothing more than an arrangement of notes and rhythms," others maintain that music always bears meaning, that the infinitely varying ways in which those "notes and rhythms" are arranged have everything to do with establishing what music means. For example, the music theorist Nicholas Cook wrote:

> To talk about music in general is to talk about what music means — and more basically, how it is (how it can be) that music operates as an agent of meaning. For music isn't just something nice to listen to. On the contrary, it's deeply embedded in human culture. . . . People *think* through music, decide who they are through it, express themselves through it.[45]

For Warren, music by itself can't mean anything; words are required. But a moment's reflection may cause one to rethink that faulty premise. If one listens to a guitarist or pianist improvise over a blues progression, that music has meaning. Even in the absence of a sung text, many listeners could observe that the musician is playing music known as the blues and could link that music to a troubled emotional state or some sort of personal misfortune. Those musical sounds have meaning within Western culture, and that meaning is not dependent on the presence of a sung text.

Another way to consider the issue of music and meaning is to think about how music is used in conjunction with television advertising. If music is to assist in marketing and selling a particular product — persuading the consumer to purchase that product — then music has to be carefully chosen or composed in order to convey just the right meaning. The music used to market a delicate perfume will differ in its sounds from the music used to sell the newest brand of beer. Similarly, one could observe that music composed for a movie soundtrack has meaning. Depending on the scene, the mood, and the plot, music may be loud or soft, consonant or dissonant, in major or minor mode, intensely rhythmic or nearly static. The musical sounds chosen, i.e., the art of orchestration, will also play an important role. The film composer, like the composer or arranger of music for advertising, will strive to write music that has just the right meaning, music that will complement the visual elements of motion pictures and television. Significantly, the music remains the same even when the movie is exported to other cultures around the world. Thus, the music retains its meaning even when the original language is supplanted by a superimposed second language.

In the examples provided here (blues, music in advertising, music for films), there is an *extramusical* dimension present — the cultural assumptions surrounding the blues, the visual aspects of either television advertising or the movie screenplay. In other music, for example a Mozart string quartet or piano sonata, there is no extramusical dimension, but one still speaks of meaning through analyzing the syntactical and structural elements of music — the musical gestures stated and subsequently developed by the composer (*intramusical* meaning). Thus, contrary to Warren, musicologists and people of average common sense alike understand that music *always* has meaning on one level or another, and is *always* more than "an arrangement of notes and rhythms."[46] If that is true, then we need to think carefully about the use of popular music in the church's worship.

Music and Meaning—Implications for Using Popular Music in Lutheran Worship

How do we relate these concepts of music and meaning back to questions of music in the church, specifically whether popular music should find a place in Lutheran worship? Some pastors and church musicians have readily approved the use of popular music in the church, but without really thinking about what this music means. One pastor, reflecting in a church newsletter on his congregation's two Sunday services—"traditional liturgical" and "contemporary"—concluded that neither is better than the other, they are merely two different opportunities, with both services including biblical readings, preaching, confession, and prayer. He sees a good deal of similarity based on *textual* matters. Musically, however, the two types of services are significantly dissimilar and invite questions and evaluation. To pretend that there are not significant differences musically between "contemporary" and "traditional" worship is to ignore reality in the hope that unacknowledged differences will not require of pastors and church musicians some very careful and discerning thought. Another Lutheran pastor concluded that it doesn't matter what musical style is used, that growing churches use a variety of styles, and that the important thing is to have the "right spirit." To say that it "doesn't matter what style is used" is for some a deeply held truism; for others it is at least a "politically correct" statement displaying the requisite sense of tolerance in twenty-first-century America. Such a statement, however, betrays either a simple naïveté with regard to the power of music, or an unwillingness to think deeply about music and how music conveys meaning and creates identity. These Lutheran pastors have taken Warren's approach and have judged "contemporary Christian music" only by the texts and not by the music, perhaps because they regard the music as "style" rather than "substance," or perhaps because either implicitly or explicitly they maintain that music has no capacity for meaning. Thus, one might hear a Lutheran pastor or musician assert that all music is a gift of God, and all styles of music can find a place in the church's worship. In that proposition there is no careful thinking regarding music and meaning. Or one might hear the more cautious Lutheran pastor or musician assert that "not all of popular Christian music needs to be avoided; some of it speaks the Word of God." But that evaluation is based solely on text, again with no consideration for musical meaning and the implications of using popular music in church.

Asking hard questions about *musical* aspects of "contemporary" worship has been rare in current Lutheran practice. For example, what does it mean when the musicians for "traditional" worship sing and play from a rear gallery, but the musicians of the "praise band" and chorus are placed front and center, as on a stage, for all to observe? What does it mean when the instrumentation of the "praise band" is identical to that of a standard rock band? What does it mean to have a drummer who emphasizes the rhythmic backbeat, the omnipresent driving force of pop music? What does it mean when the singers in the "praise chorus" are amplified in such a way that they overshadow the singers of the congregation? What does it mean when the melodic line of a "praise song" is rhythmically complex, heavily syncopated, and soloistic instead of rhythmically straightforward and congregational? Have pastors and church musicians asked such questions and considered whether popular music is a good choice as a complement to Lutheran theology and preaching, to Lutheran identity as a confessional, sacramental, and liturgical church? Or has Lutheran "contemporary worship" simply borrowed the recipe (praise band and chorus, skits, and screen) from our American evangelical and pentecostal neighbors, because we labor under false assumptions that if we don't do so "the church's doors will soon close," that we are the ones who must "bring people to Christ" through all possible means (1 Cor 9:22), including pop music?

Luther shows us a better way. From him we learn that the *purpose* of music is to proclaim the Word of God, to hold theology and music "most tightly connected" so that we might "proclaim truth" through music. Luther shows us a better way in the *practice* of music—avoiding popular music, which carries with it meanings and associations alien to the church. Luther also shows us that we are not the ones—through our attention to people's musical preferences—who bring people to the church. Rather, it is the Holy Spirit who "calls, gathers, enlightens, and makes holy the whole Christian church on earth and keeps it with Jesus Christ in the one common, true faith."[47] We need to understand and cultivate a musical practice that contributes to the proclamation of the Word of God. The Holy Spirit will do the rest, without our attempts to match popular music with perceived community preferences.

Critics might respond by observing that merely because Luther did not use sixteenth-century popular music hardly constitutes a precedent for the way the church conducts itself in early twenty-first century America, in a society that increasingly disdains the church. We might like to think that Luther faced less challenging times than we do, that the people in Luther's Wittenberg enthusiastically filled the churches, vigorously singing the new German chorales. But such was not the case; see, for example, an excerpt from Luther's 1526 sermon for the First Sunday in Advent, where Luther observed, "The gospel suffers great contempt."[48] We sometimes tend to idealize Luther and his time, failing to realize that he lived in a society that had long been poorly served by the late medieval church. While the church was arguably a powerful presence in sixteenth-century society, it had long before Luther's time ceased to be a credible theological and spiritual force in the lives of ordinary people (witness the practice of selling indulgences). But Luther didn't counter those negative factors by trying to make church more palatable through the use of popular music. Nor should we do so, especially since twentieth-century popular music is so firmly wedded to an entertainment industry that caters to an "entertain me" society.

Other critics might assert that the church must adapt itself to varied cultural settings. One hears claims that the church can "redeem" or "baptize" any cultural form or expression, e.g., pop music, for the use of Gospel proclamation. Precisely here, however, the arguments often become poorly framed, for example when one proposes that the use of pop musical expressions is no different than the use of ethnic musical expressions. But the former is a choice; the latter may well be a necessity in sung proclamation of the Gospel. That is to say, the very real need for specific ethnic musics should not be inappropriately intertwined with a baby-boomer yearning for pop musical expressions rooted in the 1960s and '70s. A Spanish-language hymnal such as *Cantad al Señor* (St. Louis: Concordia Publishing House, 1991) appropriately draws on Hispanic musical expressions in order to enable a predominantly English-speaking Lutheran church body in North America to reach out to Spanish-speaking people with sung proclamation of the Gospel. Similarly, Lutheran missionaries working in African or Asian contexts preach and teach in local languages and dialects, translate the Bible, the Small Catechism, and Lutheran hymns into those same languages, and may draw on local musical expressions as well. Such local ethnic requirements in language and music are to be expected when American Lutherans work in cultures where English-language Bibles, catechisms, and hymnals are inadequate. Drawing on ethnic musical repertories in this way is not, however, the same as providing a "praise band" in a "contemporary service" at an American Lutheran congregation that earlier on the same Sunday morning had provided a "traditional" service. Adapting ethnic musical repertories will be necessary for Gospel proclamation in some cultures. By contrast, when American Lutheran church musicians and pastors draw on "contemporary Christian music" as led by a "praise band" they cannot rationalize that choice by asserting cultural contextualization. In fact, they are simply appropriating pop music because they like the sound of the music.

Because "contemporary Christian music" uses the same musical vocabulary as twentieth-century American pop music, it *means* entertainment. While that may not be the desired outcome by well-intentioned musicians within the church, they cannot overcome the inherent associative meaning connecting "contemporary Christian music" to various strains of American pop music from the 1960s on. Nor is it sufficient to "add Lutheran words" to music drawn from the pop culture, for the music itself has meaning and proclaims an entertainment culture and a world of personal self-expression and self-identity that does not support Lutheran proclamation of the Gospel. Such music is not a worthy complement to a place (God's house) and an occasion (the Divine Service) where Christ is truly present. Such music does not conform to the confessional, sacramental, and liturgical character of Lutheranism.

Why has it been important here to consider one of Luther's guiding principles (discerning that music from the popular culture is not a good choice for Lutheran worship) at greater length? What Luther recognized instinctively about popular music is lost on some in the twenty-first century, who rely on pop music as a primary ingredient in their worship. Further, in twenty-first-century America a confessional Lutheran church body, or an individual parish within that church body, might claim doctrinal unity, or assert the presence of a single theological identity. But a single theological identity is seriously at risk when there are at least two very different, competing musical identities, most commonly expressed as "traditional" and "contemporary." We cannot conveniently ignore the fact that different kinds of music shape different theological beliefs. If we draw our music from American evangelicalism and pentecostalism, with texts and music alike bearing a meaning foreign to Lutheranism, it is difficult at best to engender a distinctly Lutheran theological identity.[49] Nor do we *need* to borrow pop music from alien religious streams, for we have a rich heritage of music, a heritage that is constantly being renewed by the music of gifted, living twenty-first-century Lutheran composers. We turn now to examine that rich heritage in greater detail by looking again to Praetorius, Schütz, and Bach as exemplary composers within the practice of Lutheran church music.

Michael Praetorius and the Chorale

Praetorius did not merely write about music in Lutheran worship, the cantio of the Divine Service. He was one of the most prolific of Lutheran cantors, composing both Latin- and German-texted music for the Lutheran service. His Latin-texted polyphonic music includes settings of the Mass, the Magnificat, a substantial repertory of Latin hymns, and Latin motets. These Latin polyphonic settings, numbering nearly four hundred compositions, constitute by any measure a considerable compositional output. That musical corpus, however, is dwarfed by the number of his German chorale settings — over thirteen hundred compositions, ranging from homophonic four-part harmonizations (such as his well-known setting of the Christmas chorale "Es ist ein Ros entsprungen") to elaborate polyphonic settings for three or four choirs.

Praetorius held appointments as organist in Frankfurt an der Oder (1587–1590) and in Wolfenbüttel (1595–1604), becoming *Kapellmeister* as well in 1604 at the court of Duke Heinrich Julius of Braunschweig-Wolfenbüttel. At the death of the duke in 1613, Elector Johann Georg of Saxony was quick to request the services of Praetorius at his court chapel in Dresden. Here Praetorius served as a kind of deputy Kapellmeister to the semi-retired Rogier Michael, during this time coming to know the young Heinrich Schütz, whom the elector also brought to his chapel on an interim basis. In all of these appointments the chorale was central to Praetorius's work as a Lutheran cantor.

Praetorius's many published settings of chorales reveal how fundamental was the practice of alternation (*alternatim*) to the singing of chorales. Various choirs of voices and instruments joined with the congregation — *alternated* with the congregation and with one another — in singing the stanzas of a given chorale, e.g., the ten stanzas of Luther's "Dear Christians, One and All, Rejoice." In alternation practice various musical forces participate in proclaiming the theology of the chorale text; thus, musical variety is built into the experience of singing sometimes lengthy hymn texts. Moreover, choirs and groups of instrumentalists can be positioned in various places throughout the church, thus surrounding the congregation with singers and instrumentalists, thereby supporting congregational singing. Praetorius provided an expansive discussion regarding the use and placement of singers and instrumentalists in his compositions in the third part of his *Syntagma Musicum*.[50]

Such alternation practices, and the physical distribution of musicians within the room, enliven the proclamation of the Gospel in sung chorales. These practices deserve to be renewed in our day, as we continue to sing the living heritage of Lutheran chorales, as well as newer hymns in the continually developing repertory of Lutheran congregational song. From Praetorius we learn the importance of chorale and hymn singing as the absolute musical center of congregational worship. Praetorius also shows us — through his compositions and their use in alternation practice — how to make such singing lively and vital, befitting the rich theology of the chorale texts of the sixteenth century.

Heinrich Schütz and the Concerto

Like Praetorius, Schütz composed an extensive body of Latin- and German-texted sacred music. Unlike Praetorius, however, Schütz was able to travel to Italy — then the center of new developments in music — on two separate occasions for compositional study. In another contrast between these two Lutheran composers of the early seventeenth century, it was Praetorius who was the prolific writer, the theorist who wrote extensively on all aspects of music theory and the musical instruments of his time.

In his early twenties Schütz was encouraged by Landgrave [Count] Moritz of Hessen-Kassel to travel to Venice for study with the famous composer Giovanni Gabrieli (ca. 1554/7–1612). In 1609 Schütz arrived in Venice for what was intended to be two years of study, subsidized by Moritz. Schütz excelled in his studies in composition and in organ playing and remained in Venice for a third year. Gabrieli died in August 1612, and Schütz returned to Moritz's court in 1613. From Gabrieli, Schütz learned the craft of sixteenth-century counterpoint in late Renaissance style, and he became acquainted with the Venetian polychoral style of composition ("polychoral" designating music for "more than one choir," such "choirs" involving singers, instrumentalists, or both).

In August 1614 Elector Johann Georg I of Saxony asked Moritz to allow Schütz to travel to Dresden and assist in providing music for the Baptism of the elector's son. At that point Johann Georg's Kapellmeister, Rogier Michael, was semiretired, and Michael Praetorius was serving as a temporary, visiting Kapellmeister. By October, Schütz had fulfilled his limited duties in Dresden and had returned to Kassel and his work in Moritz's chapel, but in April 1615 Johann Georg again asked for Schütz, this time for a period of two years. In August 1615 Schütz again went to Dresden, and by 1618 Moritz had reluctantly given up his repeated attempts to secure Schütz's return to Kassel. In Dresden, Schütz did not immediately receive the title Kapellmeister, perhaps in deference to the role of Praetorius at the electoral court. Schütz's first published sacred compositions, the *Psalmen Davids*, appeared in 1619 and certainly would have served notice that Schütz was an enormously gifted composer. The *Psalmen Davids*, reflecting his period of study with Gabrieli, are scored in polychoral fashion for two or more groups of singers and/or instrumentalists, the Dresden court chapel being at that time the most lavishly appointed musical establishment in Lutheran Germany, with twenty-seven musicians available to Schütz.

In 1628–1629 Schütz undertook a second trip to Venice, in part no doubt to escape the economic problems caused by the Thirty Years' War (1618–1648) in the German-speaking lands. While Saxony had at that point no direct involvement in the armed conflict (that would not happen until 1631), it was still the case in 1628 that Schütz's Hofkapelle musicians were forced to appeal to Johann Georg for unpaid back wages. On this second trip to Italy, Schütz encountered a quite different musical style, for this was no longer the Venice of Giovanni Gabrieli but now of Claudio Monteverdi (1567–1643). In the foreword to his *Symphoniae Sacrae I* (Venice, 1629), Schütz wrote:

> When I visited my friends in Venice, I recognized that the style of musical composition had somewhat changed, and that the old laws had been to some extent abandoned in the attempt to flatter the ears of today with new delights. I have now consigned all my

mind and strength to producing something in this new manner of composition, so that you may become acquainted with it.[51]

The new style of which Schütz wrote was exemplified by the sacred concertos of Monteverdi and Alessandro Grandi (1586–1630), which would have been current in Venice at the time of Schütz's second visit.

When we as twenty-first-century listeners think of the word "concerto," we usually think of the late eighteenth- (e.g., Mozart) or nineteenth-century concerto, where a single musician (e.g., a pianist or violinist) is opposed to, or contrasts with, a symphony orchestra, the composer typically providing the soloist opportunity to display individual musicianship and technical accomplishment. In the early seventeenth century, however, the word "concerto" had a different meaning, emphasizing the joining together ("concertare") of diverse musical forces—both voices and instruments, in various combinations. The concept of concertare/concertato/concerto was applied broadly in early seventeenth-century sacred works, including music of Gabrieli (the polychoral concerto) as well as Monteverdi. The predominant type of Baroque sacred concerto came to be the small-scale sacred concerto for one to four solo voices, basso continuo, and (frequently) solo instruments. ("Basso continuo" refers to an independent bass line that continues throughout a composition, above which the harmonic structure of the piece is improvised on a chord-playing instrument such as an organ, harpsichord, or lute.) Moreover, this type of sacred concerto typically featured a text/music relationship in which the words suggested the music, the music sensitively expressing or reflecting the affective meaning of the text. *Symphoniae Sacrae I* (1629) constituted Schütz's early involvement with the small-scale sacred concerto.

Another development unrelated to music served to confirm the importance of the small-scale concerto for Schütz. In 1631 Saxony entered the Thirty Years' War. Gradually during the 1630s the musical resources of the Dresden Hofkapelle decreased until by the end of the decade Schütz had no more than ten musicians at his disposal. In 1636 and 1639 Schütz published volumes one and two of his *Kleine geistliche Konzerte*, small-scale concertos for voices and basso continuo. Unlike the *Symphoniae Sacrae* of 1629, obbligato instrumental parts were not included, Schütz making clear in the introduction to both the 1636 and 1639 publications that "the constant perils of war" and "the wickedness of the times" permit only these "small sacred concertos" as music for the church. While Schütz was somewhat apologetic for these works, writing in the dedication to the 1639 collection, "I must confess that I am ashamed to appear before your Highness with such a small and unworthy little work,"[52] we recognize in these miniature masterworks not only the musical craftsmanship of a master composer but also the ability of one of the great Lutheran cantors to proclaim the Gospel through music. Consider Schütz's setting of John 11:25–26 in Part 2 (1639) of *Kleine geistliche Konzerte*.

In "Ich bin die Auferstehung und das Leben" (SWV 324)[53] Schütz set the familiar words of Jesus to Martha, as recorded in John 11:25–26: "I am the resurrection and the life. Whoever believes in me, though he die, yet shall he live, and everyone who lives and believes in me shall never die." Schütz scored his setting for two tenors, bass, and organ, those four musicians constituting nearly half of his complement of musicians at the Dresden court chapel in 1639. Schütz set the text twice (measures [mm.] 1–25 and mm. 25–49). The first time through only the bass sings "I am the resurrection and the life," while the two tenors focus on the text "whoever believes in me, though he die, yet shall he live" and "everyone who lives and believes in me shall never die" (ex. 3). In the first half of the concerto, Schütz reserved those most amazing words of Jesus — "I am the resurrection and the life" — for the bass alone, as if the bass was singing the "role" of Jesus (later Bach would do the same thing by assigning to the bass voice the words of Jesus in his setting of the *St. Matthew Passion*). Then in the second half of the concerto, these words are reserved for the two tenors, who proclaim them twice in duets constructed largely in the sweet sonority of parallel thirds (ex. 4). By this simple means Schütz reiterates "I am the resurrection and the life" in a musical way that claims the listener's attention but is not musically difficult or complex for the singers. With the Dresden chapel at a low ebb, he may no longer have had access to the most talented singers.

But without doubt the most striking part of Schütz's setting is how he seizes on the final part of the text: "and everyone who lives and believes in me shall never [*nimmermehr*] die." The way that Schütz repeats "nimmermehr" is simply remarkable. He shows that he understands the Gospel proclamation in this passage, the good news that makes all the difference for the believer — that his soul shall *never, never* die.[54] Schütz always repeats the word "nimmermehr" using the rhythm <eighth, eighth, quarter/eighth, eighth, quarter>, tossing the musical motive through all three vocal parts for a stunning cumulative effect, one that the listener cannot miss (ex. 5). It is Gospel proclamation at its very finest.

And that is the point of considering Schütz and his music here — as a case study in the practice of Lutheran church music. His setting of this Gospel text is neither lengthy nor complex; on the contrary, it is concise and calls for only three singers and one instrumentalist. Within those restricted and economical means Schütz found a musically interesting way to proclaim eternal life in Christ, and precisely that is the goal of music in Lutheran worship.

A second example of Gospel proclamation drawn from the works of Schütz is his setting of Luke 18:10–14, the parable of the Pharisee and the tax collector praying in the temple. As in Schütz's day and also in our one-year lectionary, this lesson (Lk 18:9–14) is the appointed Gospel for the Eleventh

H.S.VI.

Example 3. Heinrich Schütz, "Ich bin die Auferstehung und das Leben" from *Kleine geistliche Konzerte* (Dresden, 1639), mm. 1–11

H.S.VI.

Example 4. Heinrich Schütz, "Ich bin die Auferstehung und das Leben" from *Kleine geistliche Konzerte* (Dresden, 1639), mm. 21–33

Example 5. Heinrich Schütz, "Ich bin die Auferstehung und das Leben" from *Kleine geistliche Konzerte* (Dresden, 1639), mm. 41–49

Sunday after Trinity (and also for Proper 25 in Series C of the three-year lectionary). Schütz's setting, "Es gingen zweene Menschen hinauf" (SWV 444), is scored for four voices (S,S,T,B) and basso continuo.[55] The contrast between the two men in the parable could not be greater, and Schütz uses musical means to emphasize and heighten that contrast. The self-righteous Pharisee, asking nothing of God, thanks God that he is "not like other men" and enumerates his virtues in fasting and tithing. Schütz scores this part for a bass singer and provides him much text repetition, befitting the proud Pharisee intent on calling attention to his own merit. Above this self-righteous monologue, the penitent tax collector (a tenor) can only whimper his persistent prayer "God, be merciful to me, a sinner." Schütz's setting brilliantly portrays the fundamental difference between the Pharisee and the tax collector, and in so doing proclaims the truth in Christ's parable.

Johann Sebastian Bach and the Cantata

Bach's cantatas show the continuing close connection in eighteenth-century orthodox Lutheranism between concio and cantio, between Gospel text and a musical exposition of that text. Bach's cantata for Trinity Sunday, *O heil'ges Geist- und Wasserbad* ("O Holy Washing of Water and the Spirit"), BWV 165, will serve here as a case study.[56] This cantata was first performed in Weimar on June 16, 1715. The text (or libretto) of the cantata is by Salomo Franck, court poet at Weimar, and is based on the appointed Gospel lesson for Trinity Sunday, John 3: 1–15, the title of the cantata relating to verse five: "Unless one is born of water and the spirit, he cannot enter the kingdom of God." Today this lesson remains the appointed Gospel for Trinity Sunday in the one-year lectionary and in year B of the three-year lectionary.

Bach composed about 300 cantatas, of which about 200 have come down to us. While we might consider this a substantial number of works, consider that Bach's contemporaries Georg Philipp Telemann (1681–1767) and Christoph Graupner (1683–1760) composed about 1,200 and 2,000 cantatas, respectively. Bach's cantatas date primarily from his years in Weimar and Leipzig. Bach was employed in Weimar from 1708 to 1717, first as court organist and, from 1714, also as *Konzertmeister*. The latter appointment required him to provide a cantata for the court chapel on a monthly basis. About twenty of his surviving cantatas may be dated to the years 1714–1716 in Weimar, including the Trinity Sunday cantata under consideration here.

Most of Bach's sacred cantatas were composed (and older ones reworked) during his early years in Leipzig, beginning in May 1723. His appointment there included two broad areas of responsibility: 1) as cantor of the St. Thomas School he was responsible for the musical training of the students at that boarding school, and 2) as director of music for the city of Leipzig he provided for and supervised the music at four of the city churches. Bach needed to provide a cantata every week, and his efforts in that regard were particularly noteworthy in 1723–1724 and 1724–1725, when he produced two extensive (though not absolutely complete) annual cycles of cantatas. The Weimar cantata *O heil'ges Geist- und Wasserbad* was reused by Bach in Leipzig, possibly on Trinity Sunday of 1724.

One of the most interesting and helpful documents that has come down to us in Bach's own hand is a simple listing of the order of elements in the Divine Service as it was observed in Leipzig; he entered this list in the autograph score of the cantata BWV 61, *Nun komm, der Heiden Heiland* ("Now Come, Savior of the Heathen," or, as we know it today, "Savior of the Nations, Come").[57] That cantata was first performed in Weimar on the First Sunday in Advent, December 2, 1714, and repeated during Bach's early years in Leipzig, probably for the First Sunday in Advent, November 28, 1723. Bach's listing in the manuscript of BWV 61 shows us how the cantata fits into the Sunday morning service. After the Gospel, Bach notes "preluding on" (and, by implication, performance of) the "principal music," i.e., the cantata. Bach rarely used our term "cantata," using instead the term *Hauptmusik* (principal music) or simply *Musik* (the music). Following the Hauptmusik the congregation sang the Nicene Creed in Luther's hymnic version: "Wir glauben all an einen Gott" ("We All Believe in One True God"). Then the pastor preached the sermon, and after the sermon the congregation sang a hymn. Holy Communion followed; Bach notes the Words of Institution, and then preluding on [and performance of] "the music," i.e., a second part of the cantata if there was a part two, or perhaps a distinct second cantata. Thus, the cantata, or Hauptmusik, found its place after the reading of the Gospel and before the creed and sermon, secondarily during distribution of the Lord's Supper. It is useful for us to note how closely the cantata was related—by its very placement in the Divine Service—to Word and Sacrament. The sequence of Gospel/cantata/creed/sermon places musical proclamation right after the reading or intoning of the Gospel lesson for the day. The preaching, based on the Gospel, was, therefore, prepared by the Hauptmusik. The cantata was the *musical* proclamation of the Gospel; the sermon was the *spoken* proclamation of the Gospel. It is that purposeful sense of music as proclamation, linked to the Gospel, that still serves us well as a model today.

Cantata 165, *O heil'ges Geist- und Wasserbad*, consists of six sections, alternating between arias and recitatives: soprano aria, bass recitative, alto aria, bass recitative, tenor aria, and the concluding chorale verse. ("Recitative" is a text-music relationship providing for declamation of prose texts, typically accompanied only by basso continuo, with little or no text repetition. "Aria" is a text-music relationship involving most often poetic texts, with instrumental accompaniment usually going beyond the basso continuo, and often featuring text repetition—as the composer allows musical considerations to take precedence over textual considerations.) It is scored modestly for strings and continuo, with bassoon playing the continuo bass line. The fourth section, the second recitative, is particularly interesting because it is an accompanied recitative, as distinct from the more usual *recitativo semplice* (simple recitative), with its accompaniment by continuo instruments only. Bach chooses accompanied recitative when he wants to highlight the text for a particular reason, a well-known example being in his *St. Matthew Passion*, where the words of Jesus are highlighted by strings joining the accompaniment.

Let's imagine ourselves in Leipzig on Trinity Sunday. We are seated in one of the two principal churches—either St. Thomas or St. Nicholas, the performance of one of Bach's cantatas normally alternating between those two churches from one Sunday to the next. The church is quite full for the three- to four-hour morning service, each church accommodating around 2,500 people, reports of full churches being common during this period in Leipzig's history.[58] The first hour accommodated those parts of the service up through the sequence of Gospel/cantata/creed. The second hour was devoted to the sermon. Depending on the number of communicants, the distribution of the Lord's Supper would last for one or two additional hours.

Imagine that we've reached the point in the service where the Gospel is intoned (or chanted), possibly to the chant formula provided by Luther in his 1526 *Deutsche Messe*. Following the Gospel the organist begins his preluding prior to the cantata, this musical interlude essentially providing an opportunity for the instrumentalists discreetly to tune up. Then we hear the beginning of Bach's cantata *O heil'ges Geist- und Wasserbad*. The text relates closely to the Gospel lesson just heard, where Jesus instructs Nicodemus, with a particular emphasis on Baptism, the cantata text reflecting especially verse five of the Gospel lesson: "Unless one is born of water and the Spirit, he cannot enter the kingdom of God." Thus, the first aria text invites listeners to reflect on the blessings of Baptism:

> O holy washing of water and the Spirit,
> Which incorporates us to God's kingdom
> And records us in the book of life!
> O flood that drowns all misdeeds
> Through its wondrous power
> And gives us new life!
> O holy washing of water and the Spirit!

The first recitative follows, with a clear presentation of Law and Gospel:

> The sinful birth of Adam's cursed offspring
> Brings forth the wrath of God, death and ruin.
> For that which is born of the flesh
> Is nothing but flesh, infected by sin,

Poisoned and contaminated.
How blest is a Christian!
In the washing of water and the Spirit
He becomes a child of blessedness and grace.
He puts on Christ
And the white silk of His innocence,
He puts on the clothing of Christ's blood, the purple robe of honor,
When baptized.

The second aria is a prayer that the Christian live out his or her Baptism throughout one's earthly life:

Jesus, who out of great love
Did provide me in baptism
Life, salvation, and blessedness,
Grant that I rejoice
And renew this bond of grace
Throughout my lifetime.

In the first three sections of his libretto the poet of the cantata text, Salomo Franck, has proclaimed Law and Gospel and taught about Baptism as the Sacrament that, in the words of the Apostle Peter, "now saves you" (1 Pt 3:21a).

Thus far we have considered only the text, but with the second recitative I want to focus not only on the text but also on Bach's music, for it is, after all, the relationship between text and music that we want to view within the historical tradition of Luther and Praetorius, especially Luther's view that "God has preached the gospel through music, too." In this accompanied recitative, Bach's music *underscores* and *intensifies* certain details of the text, a text that focuses generally on Baptism, but also alludes to the last two verses of the Gospel lesson for Trinity Sunday:

And as Moses lifted up the serpent in the wilderness, so must the Son of man be lifted up: that whoever believes in him may have eternal life. (Jn 3:14–15)

Here is the text of the second recitative:

I have indeed, my soul's Bridegroom,
Since you have born me anew,
Sworn ever to be faithful to You,
Most holy Lamb of God;
Yet I have, alas, often broken the bond of Baptism

And not fulfilled what I promised,
Be merciful, Jesus
Out of Your grace, to me!
Forgive me the sins I have committed,
You know, O God, how painfully I feel
The ancient serpent's bite;
Sin's poison corrupts my body and soul,
Grant that I by faith choose you
O blood-red [fiery] serpent likeness,
Which on the cross is lifted up
Which soothes all pain
And revives me, when all strength has vanished.

Bach's music underscores details of the text — think of Bach's music as being similar to a preacher using his voice, his cadence, his sense of rhetoric to underline and emphasize certain words or phrases (ex. 6). In the music example, note the following.

In mm. 5–6: Note how Bach uses an extensive vocal melisma to emphasize the words "hoch heil'ges" (*most holy* Lamb of God).

In m. 11: It's subtle, but when Bach gets to the word "Gnaden" (grace) he uses a dotted quarter note — the longest note value thus far in the vocal line to emphasize that key theological word. In fact, no other pitch in the vocal line is longer than this one — the note value emphasizes the word musically, just as the preacher might emphasize the word "grace" by lengthening it and increasing his volume.

In mm. 12–14: Note the dissonant intervals: the c-natural leap down to d-sharp on "Sünde" (sins), and the tritone e-natural up to b-flat on "schmerzlich" (painful).

In m. 15: On the word "Schlange" (serpent) Bach's melodic line looks (perhaps more than sounds) like the "slither" of a snake.

In m. 21: Again, note the ascending tritone d-natural to g-sharp as the singer approaches the word "Schmerzen" (pain).

In mm. 22–end: On the closing text, "when all strength has vanished" ("wenn alle Kraft vergehet"), the instruments are eliminated at the final cadence, the bass line sounding the closing tonic pitch by itself — the other instruments metaphorically *not having the strength* to conclude the movement.

R.W. XXXIII.

Example 6. Johann Sebastian Bach, *O heil'ges Geist- und Wasserbad* (BWV 165), recitative no. 2

The point is not, of course, to focus on these individual details, but rather on the totality of the movement: 1) the fact that it is an accompanied recitative, and 2) the combined impact of the various ways that Bach underscores the text—he is proclaiming the Gospel text musically in advance of the pastor doing the same thing verbally and rhetorically in his hour-long sermon.

Of course, his cantatas provide hundreds of examples of Bach employing music as a means of illustrating and enhancing the theology stated in the text. While this one recitative from a single cantata must suffice here, the fact is that almost any one of his cantatas would serve equally well to show Bach *proclaiming* the Gospel through music.

Bach and the Organ Chorale Prelude

Bach's enumeration of the elements of the Divine Service in the autograph score of cantata BWV 61, *Nun komm, der Heiden Heiland*, contains two important notations on where "preluding" preceded the singing of chorales. First, Bach indicated that the organist would provide a prelude to the hymn sung between the Epistle and Gospel, the "Gradual hymn" (*Graduallied*) that was the chief hymn of the day, often linked theologically to the Gospel lesson. Second, Bach indicated that during the distribution of Communion the organist should "alternate preluding and singing of chorales until the end of the Communion."[59] From this document we can see that, at least in Leipzig, there were defined places within the principal Divine Service (*Hauptgottesdienst*) where organ chorale preludes were expected. While the specific placement of organ chorale preludes would naturally vary somewhat from one location to the next, it is certain that the organ chorale prelude found a functional use and took on specific meaning in Lutheran Germany during the seventeenth and eighteenth centuries.

One of Bach's contemporaries, Georg Friedrich Kauffmann (1679–1735), the court organist at Merseburg (and an unsuccessful candidate for Bach's position as Leipzig Thomaskantor), composed an important collection of organ chorale preludes entitled *Harmonische Seelenlust* ("The Soul's Desire for Harmony"), which was published in Leipzig in installments between 1733 and 1740. In his preface, Kauffmann articulated a specific purpose for the chorale preludes in *Harmonische Seelenlust*:

> Since it has become the custom in numerous places to provide a short improvisation before each chorale, organists have tried to come as close as possible to the true manner which allows the melody to be heard in a clear, distinct but nevertheless artistic way, using imitation or any other [figural passages], so that [one] is gradually prepared to sing the chorale with much more devotion than if one had heard an unknown fantasy.[60]

Thus, Kauffmann advocated not only a chorale-based prelude, as opposed to a free work such as a fantasia or a prelude and fugue, but also a prelude where the chorale melody can "be heard in a clear, distinct but nevertheless artistic way" — a chorale *cantus firmus* (or hymn melody) that is readily *perceptible* and recognizable to the listener. Kauffmann demonstrated that kind of writing in his own compositions; see, for example, his setting of "Nun danket alle Gott" ("Now Thank We All Our God") from his *Harmonische Seelenlust*.[61]

Taken as an entire musical corpus, Bach's organ chorale preludes show a great variety of cantus firmus treatment, ranging from a clearly perceptible cantus firmus in a single voice, to a cantus firmus in canon between two voices, to a lightly ornamented cantus firmus where the chorale melody is very much recognizable, to a heavily ornamented chorale melody where that melody is virtually obscured. These various possibilities in the treatment of a chorale melody are well illustrated in Bach's manuscript collection of forty-six chorale preludes, the "Orgelbüchlein" (BWV 599–644), most of which date from Bach's years as organist at the Weimar court chapel (1708–1717).

From the title page of this collection it is clear that Bach was providing improvisational/compositional models for presenting the text and tune of a chorale in a concise organ setting:

> Little Organ Book . . . In which a beginner at the organ is given instruction in developing a chorale in many divers ways . . . .[62]

Consider, for example, Bach's setting of the Pentecost chorale "Komm, Gott Schöpfer, Heiliger Geist" (BWV 631), "Come, Holy Ghost, Creator Blest." Bach sounds the chorale melody (the chant melody associated with the medieval Latin hymn "Veni creator spiritus") clearly and without any ornamentation in the soprano voice (ex. 7). The bass voice emphasizes the *third* pulse in each three-note grouping within the 12/8 meter, Bach thereby reminding the listener that in this hymn we sing of the Holy Spirit — the *third* person of the Holy Trinity. Bach later expanded this "Orgelbüchlein" setting by adding a second statement of the chorale melody in the bass voice, with imitative scalar passages in the upper voices, cf. the organ chorale prelude BWV 667.

One could point to any of the "Orgelbüchlein" settings as exemplifying in some special way an aspect of theological proclamation. These organ settings by Bach illustrate the proclamatory potential of the organ chorale prelude — wordless, purely instrumental music, to be sure, but in each case conveying a specific poetic text by way of the melody traditionally associated with that text. That kind of associative communication process remains of central importance in Lutheran church music of today and will be explored in the next chapter in the context of our musical choices.

Komm, Gott, Schöpfer, heiliger Geist.

B.W. XXV. (II)

Example 7. Johann Sebastian Bach, "Komm, Gott Schöpfer, Heiliger Geist" (BWV 631), from the "Orgelbüchlein"

Beyond Bach . . . Briefly

At the beginning of this chapter I emphasized that "Luther, Praetorius, Schütz, and Bach have something to teach us historically." I also noted that Lutheran church musicians working in the early part of the twenty-first century likely will not "draw solely or even principally" on the music of those composers. But regardless of whether the twenty-first-century Lutheran church musician actively uses the chorale settings of Michael Praetorius, the small-scale concertos of Schütz, or the cantatas and organ chorales of J. S. Bach, those genres of historic Lutheran church music become for us examples and benchmarks of well-crafted music in the Divine Service, and models of music as Gospel proclamation.

Lutheran composers of our own time are the successors of Luther, Praetorius, Schütz, and Bach. Living Lutheran composers take their place in the long line of the Lutheran cantorate, and provide well-crafted music that plays its part in Gospel proclamation. Thus, I conclude this chapter by looking at select examples of music by living Lutheran composers—in two genres: hymn tunes by Carl F. Schalk (1929–) and Stephen R. Johnson (1966–), and organ hymn preludes by Kevin J. Hildebrand (1973–). These composers stand here as representative twenty-first-century Lutheran composers—heirs of a rich tradition, who continue in our own time to provide new music that proclaims the Word of God.

Just as Luther was a very capable composer of hymn melodies,[63] so also in our day Carl F. Schalk and Stephen R. Johnson are among Lutheran composers who have written well-crafted tunes and harmonizations that allow us to sing the Gospel. One of Schalk's finest tunes, FORTUNATUS NEW, sets a sixth-century text by Venantius Fortunatus, translated as "Sing, My Tongue, the Glorious Battle" and designated in current hymnals for use during Holy Week (*CW* 122, *ELW* 356, *LSB* 454). Schalk's tune is in AAB form (sometimes called "bar" form), where the second melodic phrase is identical (or nearly so) to the first. This kind of musical repetition makes the melody easier for the ear to grasp on first hearing and ultimately easier to sing. Some of the earliest Lutheran chorale melodies also repeat the first musical phrase; see, for example: "Dear Christians, One and All, Rejoice" (*CW* 377, *ELH* 378, *ELW* 594, *LSB* 556), "A Mighty Fortress Is Our God" (*CW* 200, *ELH* 250, *ELW* 503, *LSB* 656), and "O Lord, We Praise Thee" (*CW* 317, *ELH* 327, *ELW* 499, *LSB* 617). Beyond its AAB form, Schalk further unifies FORTUNATUS NEW by repeating the opening melodic and rhythmic gesture a fifth higher, and then by bringing that same gesture back in the third melodic phrase. His tune is economically constructed both melodically and rhythmically, and thus easily grasped and readily sung by the congregation.

Johnson's tune SUFFICIENTIA is a strikingly beautiful twenty-first-century melody and harmonization for one of Paul Gerhardt's (1607–1676) seventeenth-century hymn texts, translated in *LSB* 754 as "Entrust Your Days and Burdens." Here is yet another example where the composer repeats the first melodic phrase nearly exactly as the second phrase. Further, the third phrase employs melodic repetition, while the fourth phrase borrows the cadential figure from the end of the second phrase. Again, one sees the composer providing a tightly organized, melodically economical hymn tune that is highly singable.

Neither Schalk's nor Johnson's melodies spring from the world of popular music. Instead, one sees Lutheran composers creating music of and for the church, well-crafted music that finds its contextual moorings in the long history of unison vocal music for use in the church, rather than in the soloistic vocal music, accompanied by a prominent instrumental rhythmic backbeat, characteristic of pop music from the 1960s on. While one certainly can distinguish musical stylistic differences between the sixteenth-century melodies of Luther on the one hand, and the more recent melodies of Schalk and Johnson on the other, e.g., the striking flat seventh degree at the beginning of Johnson's third phrase, there is, nevertheless, a straight line of unison vocal intent and melodic craftsmanship extending from Luther to his living successors in the twenty-first century.

Kevin Hildebrand, Associate Kantor at Concordia Theological Seminary, is an active composer of organ and choral music for the church. Thus far, eight sets of *Six Hymn Improvisations* have been published,[64] as well as other collections of hymn preludes specifically designated as "easy preludes."[65] What particularly commends Hildebrand's hymn preludes is the consistent presence in each prelude of a clearly perceptible hymn melody. In a *functional* sense, such a composition announces a hymn about to be sung, or recalls a hymn sung earlier in the Divine Service. In a *theological* sense, such a composition relies on the prominent, perceptible statement of a hymn melody to bring to mind the hymn text (or at least a portion of that text) as a means of specific theological proclamation (more on this communication process in Chapter Three). Consider, for example, his setting of the tune EBENEZER for Martin Franzmann's text "Thy Strong Word" (*CW* 280, *ELH* 72, *ELW* 511, *LSB* 578). Each phrase of the hymn melody sounds clearly in the soprano voice (with a suggested solo reed registration), while a full-textured, rhythmically interesting ritornello passage precedes the first and second phrases of the melody and follows the final melodic phrase. Thus, the composer highlights the hymn melody but finds interesting textural, harmonic, and rhythmic means to do so. Hildebrand's compositions are always well crafted and stand in a long line of Lutheran organ improvisation and composition, extending from the seventeenth century to the present day.

Living Lutheran composers of hymn tunes and harmonizations, organ hymn preludes, and liturgical vocal and choral music are heirs of Luther,

Michael Praetorius, Schütz, J. S. Bach, and many others. We should not take for granted that living composers continue and extend the rich heritage of well-crafted Lutheran church music, creating hymn tunes that permit the congregation to sing the faith, and creating organ, instrumental, and vocal music that embellishes and enriches congregational song and the music of the Divine Service. Schalk, Stephen R. Johnson, and Hildebrand are representative of a large and active contingent of well-trained, living Lutheran composers who provide the means to preach the Gospel through music.

Summary

This chapter has focused on the *practice* of Lutheran church music—as defined by Luther and carried out by subsequent Lutheran cantors of the seventeenth and eighteenth centuries. Luther's practice of music retained the church's heritage of sacred music, especially the repertory of Latin chant. Simultaneously, Luther and his coworkers created a body of vernacular hymnody, the chorale, so that people could sing the Gospel in their own language. Just as he retained Latin chant, Luther also drew on the Latin polyphony of his day as an integral part of music for the Mass, Matins, and Vespers. Similarly, he encouraged composers to apply the polyphonic style of the Latin motet to settings of the new German chorales, e.g., Johann Walter's 1524 polyphonic settings of chorales. Finally, Luther discerned that the popular music of his time was not an apt choice for use within Lutheran worship.

Subsequent Lutheran cantors built on Luther's generous vision of church music. Michael Praetorius brought his understanding of alternation practice to the composition and performance of the German chorale, suggesting a variety of instruments and vocal groupings to enrich and support the congregational singing of chorales. Heinrich Schütz, like Praetorius before him, composed settings of both Latin and German texts for the Divine Service. Schütz employed the Baroque concerto as a primary musical means of proclaiming the Gospel, doing so equally well with many musicians (the polychoral concerto) and with few musicians (the small-scale concerto for solo singers accompanied only by organ). In the Leipzig service of J. S. Bach's time both the cantata and the organ chorale prelude found appointed places as agents of Gospel proclamation, the cantio that complemented the sermonic concio. Thus, from Luther to Praetorius, from Schütz to Bach, and beyond Bach to the living Lutheran composers of the twenty-first century, there is a continuum of proclamatory music, composers using the formal conventions of their time, such as concerto and cantata, and the melodic, harmonic, and contrapuntal procedures of their time to compose music that bears the Word of God to listeners—then and now.

Notes

1 LW 53, 13.
2 Ibid., 19–40.
3 Ibid., 22.
4 Ibid., 23.
5 Ibid., 24.
6 Ibid., 25.
7 LW 54, 361.
8 LW 53, 21.
9 Ibid., 25–26.
10 LW 49, 68.
11 LW 53, 36.
12 This receptiveness to both Latin and German would continue to be characteristic of Lutheran liturgy and music. Johann Spangenberg's *Cantiones Ecclesiasticae Latinae/Kirchengesenge Deudsch* (Magdeburg, 1545) was the first printed volume to provide both Latin and German monophonic music for the church year. The first half of the volume, *Cantiones Ecclesiasticae Latinae*, extends from Advent 1 through the end of the church year, providing a selection of Latin monophonic music for the major feasts of the church year. The second half of the volume, *Kirchengesenge Deudsch*, does the same, providing a selection of German-language chorales and propers from Advent 1 to the end of the church year. For more on Spangenberg's anthologies see Robin A. Leaver, "Johann Spangenberg and Luther's Legacy of Liturgical Chant," *Lutheran Quarterly* 19 (Spring 2005): 23–42.
13 LW 53, 37.
14 LW 49, 69.
15 A facsimile was published as an insert to *Jahrbuch für Liturgik und Hymnologie* 2 (1956) and 50 (2011). Though the title page of *Etlich Cristlich lider* states the place of publication as "Wittenberg," this small book was printed by Jobst Gutknecht of Nuremberg.
16 "Dear Christians, One and All, Rejoice": *CW* 377, *ELH* 378, *ELW* 594, *LSB* 556.
17 "Salvation unto Us Has Come": *CW* 390, *ELH* 227, *ELW* 590, *LSB* 555.
18 Analysis of the scriptural citations provided for each stanza of "Es ist das Heil uns kommen her" may be found in Daniel Degen, "Das Lied 'Es ist das Heil uns kommen her' von Paulus Speratus," *Jahrbuch für Liturgik und Hymnologie* 49 (2010): 148–57.
19 A facsimile was published as *Das Erfurter Enchiridion*, Documenta Musicologica, Erste Reihe: Druckschriften-Faksimiles, no. 36 (Kassel: Bärenreiter, 1983).
20 A facsimile was published as Johann Walter, *Das geistliche Gesangbüchlein "Chorgesangbuch,"* Documenta Musicologica, Erste Reihe: Druckschriften-Faksimiles, no. 33 (Kassel: Bärenreiter, 1979).
21 Joseph Herl, *Worship Wars in Early Lutheranism: Choir, Congregation, and Three Centuries of Conflict* (New York: Oxford University Press, 2004), 14–15.
22 LW 53, 63.
23 Ibid.
24 Ibid., 69.
25 Ibid., 74.
26 Ibid., 78.
27 Ibid., 81–82.
28 See Herl, pp. 8–14, for a discussion of the difficult questions regarding who — congregation or choir — sang these vernacular hymns in the *Deutsche Messe*.
29 LW 53, 90.

30 On the importance of Lutheran hymns in the sixteenth-century home see Christopher Boyd Brown, *Singing the Gospel: Lutheran Hymns and the Success of the Reformation* (Cambridge, Mass.: Harvard University Press, 2005).

31 LW 53, 324.

32 Leaver, *Luther's Liturgical Music*, 101. LW 54, 129–30, mistranslates the final part of this quotation as "and are like the song of the finch." But the finch has only one, repetitive song.

33 See Luther's letter of October 4, 1530, to Senfl: LW 49, 426–29.

34 Praetorius, *Syntagma Musicum I*, 314.

35 Walt Kallestad, *Entertainment Evangelism: Taking the Church Public* (Nashville: Abingdon Press, 1996), 10.

36 Rick Warren, *The Purpose Driven Church: Growth Without Compromising Your Message & Mission* (Grand Rapids, Mich.: Zondervan, 1995), 282.

37 James Brauer, "The Devil's Tunes," *Concordia Journal* 23 (January 1997): 2–3. See also John Bartlett, *Familiar Quotations*, 11th ed. (Boston: Little, Brown, 1937), 274.

38 The two melodies for "From Heaven Above" ("Vom Himmel hoch") are available for comparison in Leaver, *Luther's Liturgical Music*, 17. A facsimile of the Babst hymnal was published as *Das Babstsche Gesangbuch von 1545*, Documenta Musicologica, Erste Reihe: Druckschriften-Faksimiles, no. 38 (Kassel: Bärenreiter, 1988); "Vom Himmel hoch" is the fourth hymn in this 1545 hymnal.

39 LW 53, 316.

40 Nor can one invoke as historical precedent for the use in Lutheran worship of music from the popular culture the hymn melodies O WELT ICH MUSS DICH LASSEN or HERZLICH TUT MICH VERLANGEN. The former was either composed by Heinrich Isaac (ca. 1450/55–1517) or adapted by him from a folk source, Isaac's polyphonic setting accommodating the secular text "Innsbruck, ich muss dich lassen." The latter was composed by Hans Leo Hassler (1564–1612) to accommodate the secular text "Mein G'müth ist mir verwirret." Thus, both of these secular melodies have their origin in the world of art music, not in the world of popular culture. An analogue today would be taking a secular melody by the American composer Aaron Copland (1900–1990) and fitting a sacred text to that melody. That process is known as *contrafactum*.

41 Early consideration of this point of disagreement may be found in two seminal articles by Richard C. Resch: "Church Music at the Close of the Twentieth Century," *Logia: A Journal of Lutheran Theology* 2 (Eastertide/April 1993): 21–27; "Music: Gift of God or Tool of the Devil," *Logia: A Journal of Lutheran Theology* 3 (Eastertide/April 1994): 33–39.

42 Frank C. Senn, "Orthodoxia, Orthopraxis, and Seekers," in *The Strange New Word of the Gospel: Re-Evangelizing in the Postmodern World,"* ed. Carl E. Braaten and Robert W. Jenson (Grand Rapids, Mich.: Eerdmans, 2002), 153.

43 Ibid., 157.

44 Warren, 281.

45 Nicholas Cook, *Music: A Very Short Introduction* (Oxford: Oxford University Press, 1998), vi.

46 Similar to Warren's assertion, it is not possible to defend the proposition "Music is not a message; it is a messenger." (Quoted in "Singing the Church's Song," *Broadcaster: The Magazine of Concordia University, Nebraska* 88 [Summer 2011]: 11.) Because music always carries meaning, it *always* bears a message (even apart from a sung text).

47 Kolb/Wengert, SC 355–56.

48 Herl, 14.

49 An interesting historical investigation of church music and identity is Jonathan Willis, *Church Music and Protestantism in Post-Reformation England*, St. Andrews Studies in Reformation History (Aldershot: Ashgate, 2010).

50 See *Syntagma Musicum III* (part III, chapter VIII) in the English translation by Jeffery Kite-Powell (Oxford: Oxford University Press, 2004), 172–213. For a splendid recorded performance of Praetorius's music — and an aural illustration of the creative potential of alternation practice, see Paul McCreesh's imaginative recording of "Praetorius's music as it might have been heard at a Lutheran mass for Christmas morning": Michael Praetorius, *Mass for Christmas Morning*, Gabrieli Consort and Players, Paul McCreesh (Archiv 439 250-2), 1994.

51 Heinrich Schütz, *Symphoniae Sacrae I/1629*, ed. Rudolf Gerber, Neue Ausgabe sämtlicher Werke, Bd. 13 (Kassel: Bärenreiter, 1957), ix.

52 Heinrich Schütz, *Kleine geistliche Konzerte 1636/1639, Abteilung 1*, ed. Wilhelm Ehmann and Hans Hoffmann, Neue Ausgabe sämtlicher Werke, Bd. 10 (Kassel: Bärenreiter, 1963), xi.

53 Ibid., 125–33. Among available recordings of "Ich bin die Auferstehung und das Leben," see the recordings by Manfred Cordes and Weser-Renaissance Bremen: cpo 999 675-2 or 777 027-2.

54 In his notes to the recording of SWV 324 by Manfred Cordes and Weser-Renaissance Bremen [cpo 777 027-2], Werner Breig observed: "Interestingly, Schütz entered a radical suggestion for abbreviation in his hand copy (today in the Herzog-August-Bibliothek in Wolfenbüttel) of the original printed edition: after the end of the first complete exposition of the text, only the concluding >>der wird nimmermehr sterben<< is supposed to follow. Might it be that Schütz felt in retrospect that the repetition of the >>nimmermehr<< extending over many measures was too playful?"

55 Heinrich Schütz, *Sämtliche Werke*, ed. Philipp Spitta, Bd. 14 (1893; repr. Wiesbaden: Breitkopf und Härtel, 1971), 55–59. English-language octavo editions include: "The Pharisee and the Publican," ed. John Finley Williamson, no. 7473 (New York: G. Schirmer, 1931); and "Two Men Betook Themselves to Pray in the Temple," ed. Richard T. Gore, no. 98-1569 (St. Louis: Concordia Publishing House, 1962).

56 Among available recordings of this cantata is the one conducted by John Eliot Gardiner: Soli Deo Gloria, SDG 138.

57 For an English-language presentation of this document, and a photographic reproduction, see *The New Bach Reader*, 113–14. A facsimile of BWV 61 is available as Johann Sebastian Bach, *Nun komm, der Heiden Heiland BWV 61: Facsimile der Originalpartitur, mit einem Vorwort herausgegeben von Peter Wollny*, Meisterwerke der Musik im Faksimile, Bd. 3 (Laaber: Laaber-Verlag, 2000).

58 Tanya Kevorkian, *Baroque Piety: Religion, Society, and Music in Leipzig, 1650–1750* (Aldershot: Ashgate, 2007). Particularly interesting for the Lutheran church musician is the first chapter, "Experiencing the service."

59 *New Bach Reader*, 113.

60 Georg Friedrich Kauffmann, *Harmonische Seelenlust, 1733–1740*, ed. Philippe Lescat, Collection Dominantes: Facsimile Jean-Marc Fuzeau (Courlay: Fuzeau, 2002), xvii.

61 Readily available in *80 Chorale Preludes: German Masters of the 17th and 18th Centuries*, ed. Hermann Keller (New York: C. F. Peters, 1937), 94–95.

62 *New Bach Reader*, 80.

63 Leaver, *Luther's Liturgical Music*, 59–63.

64 Kevin Hildebrand, *Six Hymn Improvisations* [sets 1–8] (St. Louis: Concordia Publishing House, 1998–2011).

65 Kevin Hildebrand, *Easy Hymn Preludes for Organ, vol. 3* (St. Louis: Concordia Publishing House, 2004); *O Living Bread: Easy Preludes on Communion Hymnody* (St. Louis: Concordia Publishing House, 2005).

3

CHOICES IN LUTHERAN CHURCH MUSIC

W hat music shall we sing and play in Lutheran worship? One's understanding of the purpose of Lutheran church music (the *why* of church music) and the practice of Lutheran church music (the *how* of church music) will ultimately manifest itself in one's choices of music (the *what* of church music). This chapter considers questions of musical choices by looking at selected categories of music: congregational hymns, the organ hymn preludes that announce and comment on those hymns, and vocal and choral music—with particular attention to Gospel motets. Finally, this chapter considers the vitally important task of teaching the people in our congregations about worship and music, so that our musical choices may be heard and understood conceptually as meaningful musical proclamation within the Divine Service.

The Context for Choosing Congregational Hymns

A Lutheran hymnal of our time typically contains 600 to 650 hymns. On the one hand, that's a lot of hymns. Even if a congregation were to sing four different hymns every Sunday of the church year they would utilize only about one-third of the hymns in the book. On the other hand, the hymnal committee that had the privilege of choosing the content of the hymnal likely struggled in deciding which worthy hymns (texts and tunes) could not be included, lest the book become too thick and heavy. (For a bit of historical perspective, printed hymnals from the 1720s and '30s in Lutheran Germany often included somewhere between 900 and 1,300 hymn *texts*.) The first level of choice, therefore, belonged to the committees and editors that compiled the Lutheran hymnals that we use today. But the critical next level of choice belongs to pastors and church musicians as they choose the hymn texts and tunes to place on the lips of their people for each Divine Service. It is that act of choice that is our first concern here.

Lutheran pastors and church musicians are fortunate that their work in service planning—hymn choices being a primary part of that planning—has long been shaped and governed by two external factors: the lectionary and the church year calendar. Why is this situation "fortunate"?[1] The lectionary and the church year calendar both play a role in ensuring that we pay attention to "the whole counsel of God" (Acts 20:27), not ignoring parts of Scripture or the church year that might offend twenty-first-century sensibilities. The lectionary and the church year calendar also provide the best means of guarding against the personal favorites, agendas, or idiosyncrasies of individual pastors or church musicians. In short, the lectionary and church year provide an objective framework for preaching, for worship planning, and for our musical choices. The church year and especially the lectionary constitute an indispensable and absolutely foundational framework for music to function as proclamation.

Lectionaries

A lectionary specifies the biblical lessons that are to be read aloud in Sunday and festival worship services throughout the church year.[2] Roman Catholic as well as most Protestant church bodies in North America utilize some variant of the three-year lectionary that had its origin in the liturgical reforms of the Second Vatican Council (1962–1965), which proposed in the document "Sacrosanctum Concilium": "The treasures of the Bible are to be opened up more lavishly, so that richer fare may be provided for the faithful at the table of God's Word. In this way a more representative portion of the holy Scriptures will be read to the people over a set cycle of years."[3] The three-year lectionary, *Ordo Lectionum Missae*, was subsequently introduced in Roman Catholic churches at the start of the new church year in November 1969. In the United States, Episcopalians, Presbyterians, Lutherans, and other church bodies followed soon after with their own versions of the three-year lectionary. The Inter-Lutheran Commission on Worship (ILCW), for example, published its version of the three-year lectionary in 1973. The *Revised Common Lectionary*, dating from 1992, is yet another revision of the 1969 Roman Catholic lectionary.

Among Lutheran bodies neither the 1973 lectionary of the Inter-Lutheran Commission on Worship nor the 1992 *Revised Common Lectionary* has necessarily been adopted in full. The production of any new Lutheran hymnal provides the possibility to further revise, amend, or perhaps merely tweak either the 1973 ILCW lectionary or the 1992 *Revised Common Lectionary*. That was the case, for example, with the 2006 *Lutheran Service Book* of The Lutheran Church—Missouri Synod, where the *Revised Common Lectionary* served as the basis of the three-year lectionary, but with changes primarily to the choice of Old Testament lessons, where "an even closer association with the Gospel [lesson] was pursued . . . [as well as] more narrative Old Testament texts to provide balance with the larger number of prophetic readings in the three-year lectionary."[4] The 2008 *Christian Worship Supplement* of the Wisconsin Evangelical Lutheran Synod includes a "Supplemental Lectionary" that "provide[s] an alternate set of readings for the First and Second Lessons in the three-year lectionary. These supplemental readings coincide thematically with the Gospel Lessons." Thus, that lectionary strives for a very high degree of congruence among the three lessons, with each second lesson aiming to connect with the Gospel lesson, rather than the second lessons being semicontinuous readings ("lectio continua") from various New Testament Epistles, which is typical of the three-year lectionary.[5] Lutheran bodies such as The Lutheran Church—Missouri Synod, the Wisconsin Evangelical Lutheran Synod, and the Evangelical Lutheran Synod have continued to provide as well the historic one-year lectionary series "of the Epistle and Gospel readings used by Luther and countless Christians for generations."[6] The one-year series continues to be preferred by some pastors, who emphasize the catechetical value of hearing the same lessons year after year.

Regardless of which lectionary is chosen for use in a particular congregation, the lectionary has the potential to provide an overall sense of unity for all aspects of the worship service on any day of the church year. Just as in Bach's day the lectionary provided a context for the cantata (the cantio) and the sermon (the concio), so also in our day it is the lectionary that can provide the basis for the sermon, the hymns, the organ music based on hymns, and the vocal and choral music. The lectionary is central, with all other concio and cantio growing outward from it, like a series of concentric circles (fig. 1). More precisely, God's Word is at the core of worship, with preaching and music (concio and cantio) seeking to explicate, explore, expound, and expand upon God's inspired, inerrant Word—one of His gifts when we gather for His Divine Service to us. The task now is to demonstrate how the lectionary provides a foundation for our musical choices, how our musical choices grow out of the appointed readings and ideally contribute to a highly unified sense of theological proclamation for each Sunday and festival of the church year.

Hymn Choices

Let us consider the First Sunday in Lent. The appointed Gospel lesson in each year of the three-year lectionary, as well as in the historic one-year lectionary, is the account of Jesus being led into the wilderness immediately after His Baptism, there to fast for forty days and forty nights before undergoing a series of temptations by the devil. Each of the synoptic

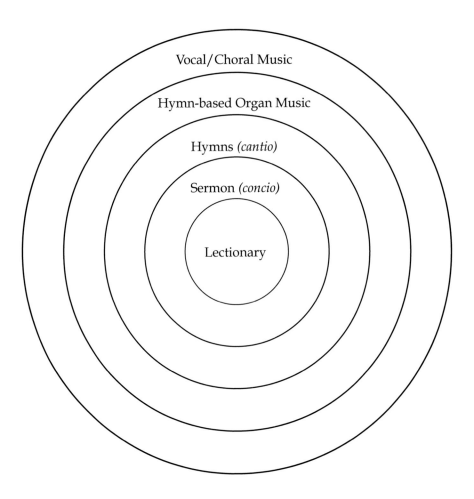

Figure 1. Central position of Scripture (lectionary) as the determinant of related service music

Gospels records this event; thus, the accounts by Matthew, Mark, and Luke provide the Gospel readings for Series A, B, and C, respectively, as is the usual procedure in the three-year lectionary.

The customary Hymn of the Day for this Sunday is Luther's "A Mighty Fortress Is Our God," the first and third verses giving us the opportunity to reflect on the devil, his temptations, and the blessings that are ours because Jesus overcame the devil's temptations. I quote from stanza one of Luther's hymn:

> The old evil foe
> Now means deadly woe;
> Deep guile and great might
> Are his dread arms in fight;
> On earth is not his equal.

And stanza three:

> Though devils all the world should fill,
> All eager to devour us,
> We tremble not, we fear no ill;
> They shall not overpow'r us.
> This world's prince may still
> Scowl fierce as he will,
> He can harm us none.
> He's judged; the deed is done;
> One little word can fell him.

Stanza one acknowledges the devil's power, but stanza three proclaims the defeat of Satan by Jesus.

Singing Luther's hymn after the Gospel lesson on the First Sunday in Lent provides us an opportunity not only to reflect on that lesson but to *proclaim* the good news that Jesus has done for us what we can never do for ourselves — resist all of the devil's assaults and temptations. In our corporate proclamation we sing:

> He can harm us none.
> He's judged; the deed is done!

The idea is not that we simply repeat the Gospel lesson; rather, we expand on the lesson, we apply it to our lives, and as a congregation we proclaim a message of hope and victory through our Savior, Jesus Christ.

Another congregational hymn that fits well for Lent 1 is "Triune God, Be Thou Our Stay" (*CW* 192, *ELH* 18, *LSB* 505). In that hymn we ask God to "Keep us from the evil one," and we paraphrase Ephesians 6:11:

Let us put God's armor on,
With all true Christians running
Our heav'nly race and shunning
The devil's wiles and cunning.

Thus, the lectionary with its Gospel lesson is at the center of the Divine Service. That lesson will often serve as the basis for the sermon (concio) and for the sung hymnic proclamation of the congregation (cantio). Referring back to Luther, the goal is for music to be "tightly connected" to theology, so that music might "proclaim truth."

When that kind of tight connection proves elusive, when one cannot identify a hymn text that is closely related to one or more of the biblical lessons specified by the lectionary, one looks then to the seasonal content of the church year. During the Epiphany season, for example, it is not always possible to identify hymn texts that specifically complement the lectionary readings. But one can continue to look to the Epiphany section of the hymnal for appropriate seasonal hymns. Similarly, the riches of Easter hymns are appropriately sung throughout the entire *season* of Easter (seven Sundays). The long season after Pentecost (the so-called "green season") sometimes presents challenges in identifying hymn texts that closely complement the appointed scriptural texts for a given Sunday. In addition to topical hymns, e.g., hymns on justification, sanctification, trust, or prayer, one can continue to choose, for example, hymns of invocation of the Holy Spirit (Pentecost Sunday by itself will not accommodate all of the riches in that category of the hymnal). The "green season" also provides an opportunity to sing hymns that focus on Baptism and the continuing "present-tense" meaning of the baptismal life ("daily a new person is to come forth and rise up to live before God in righteousness and purity forever."[7]). Similarly, the Sundays after Pentecost provide an opportunity to mine the Lord's Supper section of the hymnal for hymns to be sung during the distribution of the Lord's body and blood. In short, even the most careful worship planning cannot always lead to hymn texts that provide a seamless connection to one or more of the lectionary readings. But the seasonal rhythm of the church year provides additional guidance in hymn selection from Advent through Trinity Sunday, and the long "green season" provides opportunities to sing of the person and work of Christ and of His presence with us in Word and Sacrament.

Organ Music Based on Hymns

Organ music, and other textless instrumental music, has long been a part of the Lutheran tradition of church music, and this category of music also participates in theological proclamation. But absent a text, how is that possible? The hymn, which is both a textual and a musical expression, plays an intermediary role in linking organ hymn preludes (purely musical in nature) to lectionary readings (purely textual in nature). As both a musical and a textual expression, the hymn stands between an organ prelude and a lectionary reading, the hymn pulling those two entities toward each other so that they can stand in a meaningful relationship one to the other, the purely musical expression thus being able to comment on the lectionary reading. In this linked continuum, organ music has the capacity to proclaim specific theological meaning. For example, an organ setting of the hymn "A Mighty Fortress Is Our God" has the capability of triggering in the mind of the listener a recall of both the text of this particular hymn and, in turn, its associated theological content — perhaps, for example, the references to the devil in stanzas one and three, as considered above in the Gospel lesson appointed for Lent 1. What happens very naturally — really without our thinking much about it — is a sophisticated kind of associative communication process.[8] The perception of a well-known hymn melody leads to a recall of the associated hymn text, which leads the listener to a recognition of the theological content proclaimed by that hymn text, which itself is standing in relationship to the lectionary readings for a specific day in the church year. Thus, there is a continuum linking organ setting→to hymn melody→to hymn text→to lectionary reading, which in turn prompted the selection of that hymn, and consequently the selection of that organ hymn prelude.

It is important to understand that the more clearly perceptible the hymn melody, the greater the potential that this associative communication process will take place. Further, such a communication process assumes and is dependent upon a group of participants who have internalized a common heritage of hymn tunes and texts. In fact, this prerequisite is not only possible but likely in the life of the Lutheran parish at worship, particularly in a parish where the program of catechesis has included the study (and singing) of our heritage of Lutheran hymns — a hymn repertory extending from Luther up to and including the living poets and composers of our own day.

What are the practical aspects of linking organ music→to hymns→to lectionary readings? As much as possible, organists should play music based on the hymns selected for a particular service. Further, as much as possible, those organ settings should feature the hymn melody in a prominent and perceptible way. Our parishioners are best served by organ settings that present the hymn melody clearly; such functional music has more value within the worship service than free organ works not based on a chorale or hymn. There is, of course, no shortage of such chorale- and hymn-based organ settings, and no shortage of well-crafted settings that are nonetheless easily accessible to keyboard musicians of even modest ability.[9]

Pastors and organists should choose hymns purposefully on the basis of their textual ability to complement the readings appointed in the lectionary for each Sunday. Planning should take place well in advance, working by season of the church year, so that the organist has the opportunity to locate and learn organ settings based on the hymns for each Sunday. Sometimes hymns may be chosen with one eye toward availability of organ settings. Specifically, where two or more equally viable hymn texts are available to complement the lessons for a particular Sunday, one hymn tune may offer significantly greater possibilities from the organ literature. Here, cooperation of pastor and organist in hymn selection can pay dividends if the hymn is to fulfill an intermediary role in linking hymn-based organ music to lectionary and church year, thus allowing the organ music to play its part in theological proclamation.

What about the people sitting in the pews? Given the pervasive role of music as mere background in our society, one might ask whether it is realistic to expect that members of a congregation will use the times of organ music in the worship service as opportunities for directed reflection—thinking about the appointed lessons and the theological content of a particular day or season of the church year. Is it realistic to expect that members of a congregation will know a repertory of hymns so well that they make the mental connection from a well-known tune to its associated text? The answer to both questions depends in part on the catechetical traditions within a given parish, but also on whether organist and pastor take the time to acquaint parishioners with the concept that music in the church plays its part in the proclamation of the Gospel. We can point out to the members of our congregations that even textless organ music can be an expression of specific theological meaning and purpose, rather than mere background music before the service or during the offering. We don't want them to focus on us as musicians, nor on the music itself (as would be the case at a concert or recital). Rather, with hymnals in hand, parishioners could read the hymn text on which the organ setting is based, allowing that text to comment on the lessons for the day. We need to suggest this possibility to our parishioners by making continuing use of educational forums and other types of congregational meetings as opportunities for demonstrating the purpose and meaning of music in the Divine Service. Take people into the balcony or nave; play a short chorale or hymn prelude with a clearly perceptible hymn melody. Suggest that one might use such a prelude as a time to read the hymn text and think about its meaning. Stress that unlike a recital or concert, where one listens to music for its own sake, organ music in the Divine Service is carefully chosen for the specific purpose of contemplating the hymns and readings for the day. Demonstrate the connections and unity of approach among (in this order) readings, hymns, and organ music. Through this approach, congregational members can become increasingly aware of the proclamatory purpose of music in the Divine Service. The response I have met with most frequently from members of parishes where I have done such work is: "I've never thought about it in that way, but it makes sense." One parishioner remarked to me a week after such an educational session in the balcony: "I tried your advice this morning by reading the hymn text while you played the prelude; it made my worship experience so much richer, and when it came time to sing that hymn I did so with greater understanding." As a church musician I've never forgotten that moment, and I continue to believe that we owe our parishioners nothing less than music making that is not only done well, but done for the specific purpose of Gospel proclamation. In that way cantio stands alongside concio, in the role that Luther and Praetorius envisioned for music in worship.

A reasonable question might be, why the emphasis on the organ? What about the piano or the acoustic guitar? Might not an overemphasis on the organ lead to lack of variety in worship music? It was during the seventeenth century that the organ began to find a role in introducing and supporting hymn singing in Lutheran Germany, though the specific function of the organ and frequency of its use differed very much from one location to the next. Even in the first half of the eighteenth century in Bach's Leipzig the organ was not used to accompany every hymn. Nevertheless, over the course of the last four centuries the organ has come to occupy a prominent place in Lutheran worship. Why should that be so? First, as the organ developed during the sixteenth and seventeenth centuries it came to be a flexible instrument, one where the organist could turn off various sets of pipes by means of "stops" controlled from the player's key desk. Thus, unlike the older fifteenth-century "Blockwerk" organs (essentially an undivided principal chorus), pitch levels, and therefore volume, could be varied. Further, this increasingly flexible instrument was controlled by a single musician, a considerable practical and economic advantage.[10] Second, from the seventeenth century to the present time, Lutheran composers have developed a very large (and continually growing) repertory of organ chorale and hymn preludes designed specifically to introduce and comment on the chorales and hymns chosen for congregational singing within Lutheran worship. While some composers of the late twentieth and early twenty-first centuries have also written hymn preludes for piano, that repertory is dwarfed by the historically large and continually growing repertory of chorale and hymn preludes for organ, some of which, composed for manuals only, also work perfectly well at the piano. Third, and perhaps most significantly, the organ has come to be associated and identified very much with the church. While concert halls increasingly include fine pipe organs, the organ is still identified as a "churchly" instrument, and that in itself is a good reason for the organ still to be the instrument of choice within Lutheran worship.

Vocal and Choral Music

In many Lutheran congregations choral music still tends to be identified primarily with the anthem, a choral genre originating in the turbulent times of sixteenth-century England, when the church in England vacillated between separation from the Roman Catholic Church and full embrace of the Roman church with its Latin-language liturgy. The anthem, early examples being those of Thomas Tallis (ca. 1505–1585), was the English-language equivalent to the Latin motet, the anthem intended for use in the English-language liturgies of the Church of England. The word "anthem" has continued to be applied to English-language choral music with sacred text for use in the church, and in many Lutheran congregations it remains true that the primary purpose of the choir is to sing an anthem on an every-Sunday basis (at least from September through May or June). Such anthems may be chosen carefully to complement the appointed lectionary readings, e.g., Tallis's "If Ye Love Me" (John 14:15–17) for Easter 6 in Series A of the three-year lectionary and for Pentecost Eve in all series. Or anthems may be chosen on the basis of the church year calendar. As with careful hymn selection based on the lectionary and church year calendar, there is no doubt that choral music in the anthem genre has the potential to contribute to the primary purpose of Lutheran church music — proclamation of God's Word.

In some Lutheran parishes, however, the rather exclusive focus on the choral anthem has served to limit the choir's participation in other musical aspects of the Divine Service, for example, singing hymn verses and the appointed psalm in alternation with the congregation. The psalm in particular is still neglected by too many Lutheran congregations — treated as a dispensable part of the Divine Service, though all Lutheran service books from the 1978 *Lutheran Book of Worship* on have pointed the psalms for singing with psalm tones. Indeed the 1993 *Christian Worship: A Lutheran Hymnal* also provides an antiphon (text and melody) for each of the psalms included in that book, as does *Christian Worship Supplement*.

The Gospel Motet

Lutheran composers and choirs of the early twenty-first century would do well to focus on another genre that has been largely neglected in current practice, the Gospel motet. While the Lutheran church musician who practices careful service planning can certainly identify anthems that speak to the lectionary readings for particular Sundays and festivals, the Gospel motet is actually composed for the sake of complementing specific lectionary readings, with composers sometimes writing cycles of Gospel motets for the church year or portions thereof. The advantage of the Gospel motet is that it provides direct musical proclamation of a selected verse or verses of a Gospel lesson, underscoring and emphasizing the core of that lesson. A Gospel motet could be placed directly after the reading of the Gospel and before the Hymn of the Day, functioning in a way similar to Bach's cantatas (the *musical* proclamation of the Gospel), though the Gospel motet is brief and much less demanding musically than the typical eighteenth-century cantata.

In fact, the seventeenth-century Gospel motet is a predecessor of the sacred cantata in Germany. In seventeenth-century Germany the Gospel motet was one category of the text-motet or *Spruchmotette*, literally the motet that presented "sayings," i.e., passages or sentences. Such motets were often known as "Kernsprüche," meaning that they presented "core sayings," core scriptural passages from, for example, the Gospel lessons (thus, the Gospel motet). Composers of cycles of Gospel motets for the church year include Philipp Dulichius (1562–1631), Andreas Raselius (ca. 1563–1602), Christoph Demantius (1567–1643), Melchior Vulpius (ca. 1570–1615), and Melchior Franck (ca. 1579–1639), among others.[11]

While these historic repertories of Gospel motets certainly remain useful, so do Gospel motets composed by twentieth- and twenty-first-century Lutheran composers. Consider, for example, Jan Bender's (1909–1994) Gospel motet entitled "Begone, Satan,"[12] which sets Matthew 4:10, part of the Gospel lesson (Mt 4:1–11) for Lent 1 in Series A of the three-year lectionary, and in the historic one-year series:

> Then Jesus said to him, "Begone, Satan! For it is written, 'You shall worship the Lord your God and him only shall you serve.'"

This accessible composition for unison voices sets this Scripture verse very expressively in a recitative-like manner, and follows with the hymn verse cited earlier as appropriate for Lent 1, "Jesus Christ, Be Thou Our Stay," as a middle section, after which the Scripture verse recitative is repeated to conclude the motet. The dissonant, ugly, directionless figuration that opens and closes the recitative section (ex. 8) suggests the devil, that "adversary [who] prowls around like a roaring lion, seeking someone to devour" (1 Pt 5:8). When Jesus addresses Satan directly with the divine command "Begone," Bender utilizes the descending interval of the tritone (G-sharp to D), the tritone regarded from the Middle Ages on as the most dissonant of intervals and referred to as the "diabolus in musica" (the devil in music). Then as Jesus says "You shall worship the Lord your God and Him alone shall you serve," the solo vocal line rises diatonically from F to D, the highest pitch occurring very deliberately on the word "Him," God alone being the one who is to be served (Dt 6:13). In sixteen brief measures the composer provides music that truly comments on and proclaims this Gospel lesson for Lent 1.

The performance possibilities in this Gospel motet offer the kind of musical flexibility that is much to be desired in vocal/choral music for the

Begone, Satan

Matt. 4:10 RSV
From the Gospel for Invocavit
The First Sunday in Lent

JAN BENDER
Opus 32, No. 10

Single: Then Je-sus said to him: "Be-gone, Sa-tan! be-gone.

Sa-tan! be-gone, for it is writ-ten: 'You shall

(Ped.)

(Single ad lib.)

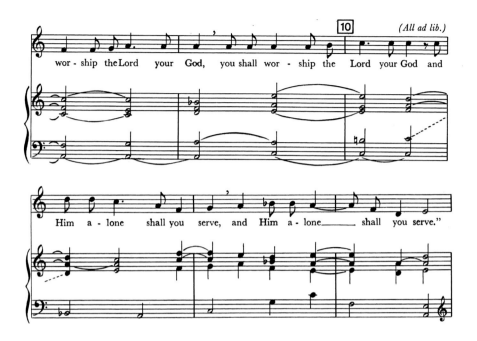

Example 8. From Gospel motet "Begone, Satan" by Jan Bender 1966, © 1994 Concordia Publishing House. Used by permission.

church. First, a choir is not necessary; a solo voice works as well. Second, either organ or piano may be used for the accompaniment. Finally, one could assign the hymn verse to the congregation, after which the choir or soloist repeats the sixteen-bar recitative section of this Gospel motet. This setting is very well crafted, presenting a "core saying" (*Kernspruch*) excerpted from this particular Gospel lesson for Lent 1. Sung immediately after the reading of the Gospel lesson, this composition provides an excellent opportunity for music to "proclaim truth."

Carlos Messerli suggests that the Gospel motet be used as part of the Gospel proclamation, not, as I have suggested here, to be sung immediately after the reading of the Gospel lesson.[13] While the hymn interpolation in Bender's "Begone, Satan" suggests to me placing that motet after the complete spoken Gospel lesson, there are other examples of the Gospel motet that would work precisely as Messerli suggests. For example, consider Knut Nystedt's (1915-) "This Is My Beloved Son," part of the Gospel lesson (Mt 17:1-9) for the Transfiguration of Our Lord, in both Series A of the three-year lectionary and in the one-year lectionary.[14] Nystedt sets only verse five of this Gospel lesson, with little text repetition. Thus, the pastor could proclaim verses 1–4, the choir (and organ) entering immediately to proclaim verse 5, and the pastor completing the proclamation of this Gospel lesson by reading verses 6–9. The impact of God the Father's words in verse five is heightened by means of Nystedt's musical setting. And this setting, like Bender's Gospel motet, exemplifies well-crafted vocal music for the church. Most of the vocal writing is for unison voices, supported by a harmonically interesting, sustained organ part (ex. 9). As Nystedt closes this brief setting he does so in accessible three-part choral writing—for soprano, alto, and baritone. A small choir would have no difficulty in learning this setting. Such vocal music is Gospel proclamation at its functional, liturgical best.

We need living Lutheran composers to provide more Gospel motets similar to Bender's "Begone, Satan" and Nystedt's "This Is My Beloved Son" — brief compositions, well crafted for the small choir, and providing a powerful musical proclamation of the Gospel. See, for example, Carl Schalk's *Scenes from the New Testament*, six Gospel lessons with settings by Schalk.[15] Lutheran composers willing to provide such functional, proclamatory music for the church would benefit from studying Messerli's suggested cycles of Gospel motet texts for all three series of the three-year lectionary.[16]

Musical Choices — Are They Meaningful to the Congregation?

Imagine that each Divine Service is carefully planned by pastor and church musician, with the lectionary (God's Word) at the center of every service. The sermon is always based on the lectionary readings (most often on the Gospel), and as far as possible the congregational hymns are related

This Is My Beloved Son

Matthew 17:5
From the Gospel for the
Transfiguration of Our Lord

KNUT NYSTEDT, 1964

Example 9. From Gospel motet "This Is My Beloved Son" by Knut Nystedt
© 1965, 1993 Concordia Publishing House. Used by permission.

to the appointed lectionary readings and the seasonal rhythm of the church year calendar. Organ music is most often based on the congregational hymns. The choir or a vocal soloist sings the appointed psalm in alternation with the congregation, and sometimes sings hymns (especially longer ones) in alternation as well. Often the choir will supply further proclamation of the Gospel by singing a Gospel motet. Pastor and church musician work collaboratively toward the goal that Luther articulated: theology and music being "most tightly connected" so that music "proclaims truth."

Is it likely that the congregation perceives this theological and musical unity in each Divine Service? At one level the answer is yes, for the unity is so clear and may be underscored and alluded to in the pastor's sermon. There is a core meaning for each Sunday and festival in the church year, and that core meaning becomes clear as each Divine Service, with its gifts of Word and Sacraments, unfolds.

Yet it is also worth emphasizing that the Lutheran understanding of worship as God's Divine Service to His people, and the Lutheran understanding of music as proclamation of God's Word, needs to be a part of catechesis in every Lutheran parish. These topics need to be *taught* at all levels—Sunday school, confirmation classes, new member/adult instruction classes, and regular high school and adult education classes. Certainly there is much to teach and much to learn. The Lutheran heritage of hymnody, for example, provides endless topics for teaching, at all levels of parish life. Study the hymn texts of Martin Luther, Philipp Nicolai, Paul Gerhardt, Martin Franzmann, Jaroslav Vajda, or Stephen Starke. *Sing* those hymns in class. Help the people to think of those hymns as prayers for use in the home, the hymnal being a home prayer book as well as a church song book. Lutheran worship, liturgy, and music taken together offer almost limitless topics for study within the parish—study that will increase people's understanding of the "tight connections" between Lutheran theology and our choices of Lutheran music.

Summary

This chapter has explored how one's understanding of the purpose of Lutheran church music (the *why* of church music) and the practice of Lutheran church music (the *how* of church music) is realized by one's choices of music: *what* the pastor and the church musician choose to place on the lips of their people as congregational song, *what* vocal and instrumental music is chosen for each occasion when God's people gather to receive His gifts in Word and Sacraments. The lectionary and the church year serve as important determining factors for our choices, our work being graphically conceptualized by a series of concentric circles, with the lectionary at the center and musical choices emanating from that core of God's Word.

Hymn *texts* chosen for a particular occasion may relate to lectionary readings, sermon, the church year, or some combination of those contextual determinants. Hymn *tunes* provide the means for linking hymn-based organ music to the meaning of hymn texts, which in turn relate back to the lectionary readings. Vocal and choral music, especially the genre of the Gospel motet, provides yet another musical means of proclaiming the lectionary readings and centering each Sunday's music on those lessons, thus linking musical choices to the central purpose of Lutheran church music: "God has preached the gospel through music too."

Notes

1   For an opposing point of view see Philip M. Bickel's "The Lectionary Captivity of the Church . . . or Ten Reasons to Kick the Lectionary Habit," *Worship Innovations* (Winter 1997): 6 ff.

2   For a valuable history of lectionaries in Christian worship, see John Reumann, "A History of Lectionaries: From the Synagogue at Nazareth to Post-Vatican II," *Interpretation* 31 (1977): 116–30.

3   Ibid., 128.

4   Arthur A. Just Jr., "The Lectionary Committee of *Lutheran Service Book*," *Journal of the Good Shepherd Institute* 7 (2006): 62.

5   *Christian Worship Supplement* (Milwaukee: Northwestern Publishing House, 2008), 6. The lists of readings for years A, B, and C are found on pages 80–82.

6   Ibid, 60.

7   Kolb/Wengert, SC 360.

8   I explore these concepts in greater detail in Daniel Zager, "On the Value of Organ Music in the Worship Service," *The Diapason* 79 (June 1988): 18–19.

9   For example, the following published series of organ hymn preludes: *The Parish Organist*, 12 vols. (St. Louis: Concordia Publishing House, 1953–1966); *Preludes for the Hymns in Worship Supplement*, 4 vols. (St. Louis: Concordia Publishing House, 1971–1973); *Concordia Hymn Prelude Series*, ed. Herbert Gotsch and Richard Hillert, 42 vols. (St. Louis: Concordia Publishing House, 1982–1986); and *Hymn Prelude Library*, ed. Kevin Hildebrand (St. Louis: Concordia Publishing House, 2012–   ).

10 Pipe organs need not be large or financially prohibitive for an individual parish. Further, they last much longer than electronic organs, whose components will, like those of computers or televisions, eventually be irretrievably compromised. On the subject of pipe organs for churches, see Bryan Gerlach, "Pipe Organ Sticker Shock and Economic Insights," *Cross Accent: Journal of the Association of Lutheran Church Musicians* 8 (Fall 2000): 24–27. Where even a small or used pipe organ is beyond the means of the small parish, an acoustic piano will provide harmonic and rhythmic support for congregational singing.

11 For useful historical background on the seventeenth-century tradition of Gospel motets in Germany, see chapters three and four of Carlos Messerli, "The *Corona Harmonica* (1610) of Christoph Demantius and the Gospel Motet Tradition" (PhD diss., University of Iowa, 1974). Among available recordings of seventeenth-century Gospel motets, see the recording by Manfred Cordes and Weser-Renaissance Bremen of motets by Philipp Dulichius (cpo 777 352-2).

12 Jan Bender, "Begone, Satan," Gospel Motets for Equal Voices, no. 98-1848 (St. Louis: Concordia Publishing House, 1966).

13 See Carlos Messerli, "The Gospel Motet for Today: Looking Backward to Expand Future Choral Possibilities in Worship," in *This Is the Feast: A Festschrift for Richard Hillert at 80*, ed. James Freese (St. Louis: MorningStar Music Publishers, 2004), 101.

14 Knut Nystedt, "This Is My Beloved Son," no 98-1805 (St. Louis: Concordia Publishing House, 1965).

15 Carl Schalk, *Scenes from the New Testament: Twelve Motets for SATB Voices and Lector* (Minneapolis: Augsburg Fortress, 2009).

16 See Messerli, "The Gospel Motet for Today," 104–20.

CONCLUSION

What Do We Ask of Lutheran Church Music?

The ongoing debates about Lutheran worship and music suggest that if three authors were each asked to write a short book entitled "Lutheran Church Music," the result would likely be three very different books with quite varying ideas and agendas concerning music in Lutheran worship. Ideas and agendas ultimately depend on what we ask of Lutheran church music, and there is much diversity today in what is asked (and expected) in this area.

Some might ask that Lutheran church music be composed, improvised, and performed in the stylistic languages of today's popular music, so as to reach people via the musical worlds where they already live, thus providing an immediacy of recognition that permits a high level of comfort to strangers entering the alien world called "church." Still others might ask that Lutheran church music be contextualized for specific generational groupings.

Some might ask that Lutheran church music pay more attention to the relationship between music and human emotions. The question may be phrased something like this: "How do you, as a church musician, make a connection with the emotions of the people in the pews?" The pastor who asked me this question referred to the music of the Russian composer Serge Rachmaninoff (1873–1943). For that pastor the beautiful melodies and lush romantic harmonies of Rachmaninoff's music created a strong emotional response, and he used that as an example to ask how church music might do something similar. I too love Rachmaninoff's music, and not infrequently it affects me emotionally. But my reply to that pastor reminded him that many people are left completely cold by Rachmaninoff's music. Perhaps Western art music in general doesn't move them. Or perhaps they prefer Bach, or Mozart, or Italian opera, but they find in Rachmaninoff an excess of romanticism that hardly has the power to move them emotionally. Music *does* act on the emotions, but different types of music affect different people in different ways. Further, to complicate matters, music that moves me emotionally on one occasion may fail to move me at another time. Nor is this necessarily predictable. Music affects individuals, and it does not necessarily affect them in predictable or consistent ways. I may be in the mood for Rachmaninoff on one day but find myself preferring the music of the jazz pianist Fred Hersch the next. That's the changeable (and fickle) nature of human emotions.

In the context of debates about music in Lutheran worship the question of emotions often presupposes that so-called "contemporary" worship music reaches a deep emotional level that the so-called "traditional" music of the church does not. "Contemporary" worship music, we are told, is music that "touches the heart." But music of any type works on individuals — some will be moved, some will not. For example, on All Saints Sunday, I can't assume that everyone in the congregation is moved deeply by singing "For All the Saints." And the All Saints Day will come again when that text and music will move me more deeply than ever, as I recall the death of a loved one in a past year. Emotions work individually — according to individual circumstances in individual lives — not corporately.

When we choose congregational hymns, vocal and choral music, organ and other instrumental music for particular Sundays, feast days, and seasons of the church year, we choose that music *not* with an eye to whether it will move people emotionally, but with an eye toward complementing the lessons for each day. In that way the music will play its part in proclaiming the Gospel. If it is well-crafted music it will also — inevitably — move *some* people emotionally. But this is a byproduct, not the goal. I am not denying that the emotions are moved within the context of music in worship; I am asserting that this happens only at the individual level, and we should not choose music in the false hope that it will move the emotions of an entire congregation. Instead, we should choose music that plays its part in each day's proclamation. Emotion, moreover, does not lead to faith; rather, emotion is a result of faith.

Some might ask that Lutheran church music be characterized by musical variety. For example, no one instrument would predominate; one would try to include in each worship service some hymns that would be accompanied by piano in addition to others that use the organ. No one hymnal would predominate, e.g., each worship service would include a mix of newer and older hymns, some from a pew hymnal, some from a newer supplement, perhaps some drawn from the hymnals of other denominations and reprinted in the service bulletin.

Depending on what one asks of Lutheran church music, one develops ideas and agendas — concerning contemporary musical styles, or how music can be tailored to various age groupings, or how music can best move the emotions, or how a church can achieve a high degree of musical variety. Moreover, one might take the point of view that these are hardly mutually exclusive categories and therefore ask of Lutheran church music *all* of these agendas.

I ask that Lutheran church music play a role in confessing truth, in teaching the Word of God, in proclaiming the Gospel. I ask that Lutheran church music take on that proclamatory task *in a distinctly Lutheran voice*, a voice that respects our musical heritage as initially shaped by Martin Luther, a voice that finds its musical antecedents in, for example, the concertos of Heinrich Schütz, the cantatas and organ chorale preludes of Johann Sebastian Bach, the Gospel motets of Jan Bender, the hymn tunes and choral music of Carl Schalk, or the organ improvisations of Paul Manz or Kevin Hildebrand. I ask that Lutheran church music go beyond the concept of presenting musical objects — no matter how beautifully composed, improvised, or performed; musical objects are the province of the concert or recital hall. Lutheran church music, after all, is *not* the same phenomenon as the "classical music" of our concert halls. On the contrary, Lutheran church music is tightly connected with Lutheran theology and functions in specific ways, within specific functional parameters that relate to Lutheran theology and liturgy. Thus, I do not ask of Lutheran church music how to achieve emotional connections or musical variety; rather, I ask of Lutheran church music a meaningful participation in the proclamation of God's Word — hymns based on the lectionary, organ music based on hymns, and vocal/choral music in genres such as the Gospel motet. Considerations of emotional response and musical variety are secondary and will, in any event, take care of themselves quite naturally as our musical choices are based on the lectionary and consistently combine with theology to proclaim truth. "God has preached the gospel through music too," and that is what we need to ask of Lutheran church music.

FOR FURTHER READING AND VIEWING

Luther, Martin. *Liturgy and Hymns.* Edited by Ulrich S. Leupold. Luther's Works, vol. 53. Philadelphia: Fortress Press, 1965.

Brown, Christopher Boyd. *Singing the Gospel: Lutheran Hymns and the Success of the Reformation.* Cambridge, Mass.: Harvard University Press, 2005.

Herl, Joseph. *Worship Wars in Early Lutheranism: Choir, Congregation, and Three Centuries of Conflict.* New York: Oxford University Press, 2004.

Koriath, Kirby L. *Music for the Church: The Life and Work of Walter E. Buszin, with Essays by Walter E. Buszin.* Fort Wayne, Ind.: The Good Shepherd Institute; Concordia Theological Seminary Press, 2003.

Leaver, Robin A. *Luther's Liturgical Music: Principles and Implications.* Grand Rapids, Mich.: William B. Eerdmans Publishing, 2007.

Schalk, Carl F. *Luther on Music: Paradigms of Praise.* St. Louis: Concordia Publishing House, 1988.

Schalk, Carl F. *Music in Early Lutheranism: Shaping the Tradition (1524–1672).* St. Louis: Concordia Publishing House, 2001.

Singing the Faith: Living the Lutheran Musical Heritage. DVD. Richard C. Resch, Executive Producer. Fort Wayne, Ind.: The Good Shepherd Institute; Concordia Theological Seminary, 2008.

ABOUT THE AUTHOR

Daniel Zager is a musicologist and Lutheran church musician. He has served as organist and director of music for Lutheran congregations in Wisconsin, Minnesota, Ohio, Illinois, and North Carolina. He earned the BMus degree in organ performance from the University of Wisconsin-Madison, and the MA and PhD degrees in musicology from the University of Minnesota. He served as a member of the Hymnody Committee for *Lutheran Service Book* and has served as editor of *Cross Accent: Journal of the Association of Lutheran Church Musicians* (2000–2002) and of the *Journal of the Good Shepherd Institute* (2000–present). In 2000 he was appointed to the Eastman School of Music (Rochester, New York), where he serves as Associate Dean and Head of the Sibley Music Library and teaches courses related to sacred music in both the musicology department and the sacred music diploma program.